MASTER THE ART OF PLANNING LIVE EVENTS

A Small Business Owners Guide to
Build Your Brand,
Drive Revenue, and
Grow a Sustainable Business

MASTER THE ART OF PLANNING LIVE EVENTS

A Small Business Owners Guide to
Build Your Brand,
Drive Revenue, and
Grow a Sustainable Business

Anza Goodbar

Dedication

This book is a tribute to my family,
the foundation of my being and the spark for my love and courage.

A massive shoutout to my Mom
for instilling in me a love for learning and the bravery to conquer
my fears and make more meaningful contributions.

To my incredible kids, Jamal, Jared, JaZelle, and Caitlin,
you light up my life with happiness every day.

Thank you for always being there for me and believing in me,
even during my moments of self-doubt.

And, to my granddaughter, Izzy. Your presence in my life brings me so
much happiness and keeps me focused on what really matters in life.

I dedicate this book to you, and I hope it inspires you to
pursue your dreams with courage and persistence,
just as you have inspired me to do the same.

Epigraph

"The future belongs to those who believe in the beauty of their dreams."

- Eleanor Roosevelt

"If you can dream it, you can do it."

- Walt Disney

"Successful events come from careful planning, hard work, and a little bit of magic."

- Unknown

Table of Contents

Preface

*H*ey there, entrepreneurs and small business owners!

I'm thrilled to share "Mastering the Art of Planning Live Events: A Small Business Owner's Guide to Build Your Brand, Drive Revenue, and Grow a Sustainable Business" with you. As a small business owner, I understand the challenges of building a business and positioning yourself as the go-to person in your industry.

I have experienced first-hand the benefits that these tactics can bring. My passion for event planning stems from my early years working in our family business, where I learned the best practices and strategies for creating successful live events.

Throughout my career, I have witnessed the transformative power of live events in connecting businesses with their customers, partners, and stakeholders. By leveraging the right tactics and strategies, businesses can create memorable experiences that leave a lasting impression, foster relationships, and drive growth. With this wealth of experience, I am eager to share my insights and help others achieve similar success through the power of live events.

Producing live events can be overwhelming and time-consuming, especially for those who need experience or resources. There are countless details to keep track of, from monetization strategies to venue selection, logistics, marketing and promotion, and most importantly, after-event follow-up. And with the COVID-19 pandemic, the landscape of live events has changed, making navigating live events more challenging.

With over 20 years of experience in the event and hospitality industry and countless lessons learned, I wrote this book with one purpose: to empower small business owners, like you, to harness live events' full potential. By offering a comprehensive guide based on my first-hand knowledge and expertise, I aim to equip you with the tools and strategies to build your brand, boost revenue, foster valuable connections within your community, and cultivate a thriving and sustainable business. Take advantage of this opportunity to leverage the power of live events and take your business to new heights.

In this book, I cover everything from event planning basics to more advanced strategies for creating successful and memorable events. Whether you are just starting out or looking to take your business events to the next level, this guide will provide the tools and knowledge you need to succeed.

Are you ready to take your business and brand to new heights through the power of live events?

Let's explore the art of event planning and discover how to transform your events into powerful opportunities for growth, impact, and success. No longer will you settle for mediocre events! With my guidance, you will achieve excellence and create unforgettable experiences that leave lasting impressions. It's time to seize the moment and elevate your business to new levels of success.

Join me, and let's unleash the full potential of live events for your business.

Introduction

I was the girl who was always searching for something new and exciting. I was afraid to commit to one career out of fear of being bored out of my mind. I discovered my gift for teaching early on. Starting at 11, I taught women how to bake in microwave ovens at my father's appliance store.

Although I knew I'd eventually own my own business, I wanted to explore the corporate world and see what it offered. I found my strengths in organization, problem-solving, and team building, and leadership there. My constant drive to improve and find a better way of doing things eventually led me to the world of event planning.

Working in the events department of a renowned nonprofit organization, I became captivated by the transformative power of live events. This experience granted me a unique opportunity to learn the ins and outs of converting a best-selling book into a sensational arena event, accommodating over 15,000 attendees. Witnessing the impact and transformations that took place at these live experiences sparked a passion in me that I couldn't ignore.

Eager to dive deeper into event planning, I joined a leading event planning company catering to prestigious Fortune 100 clients. In this role, I constantly faced challenges and received encouragement to design, plan, and execute extraordinary events that exceeded expectations. Through these experiences, I unraveled how businesses can strategically leverage events to enhance their brand, generate revenue, and boost their bottom line—all while providing immense value to their clients.

The knowledge and expertise gained in both roles have been invaluable in shaping my understanding of the transformative potential of live events, whether it's for personal growth or corporate success.

With more than 4,000 events under my belt, in 2004, I was ready for a change. I leaped into entrepreneurship and started my own mortgage company where I used community events as a lead-generation tool.

Hosting community events had an incredibly positive effect on our business. By organizing and participating in these events, we positioned ourselves as the go-to lender for individuals with less-than-perfect credit. These gatherings not only brought us closer to our clientele but they allowed us to forge strong relationships with key industry players, such as realtors, title companies, and underwriters.

Our reputation as the preferred partner for clients facing credit challenges grew exponentially due to these collaborations. The connections we made during our events helped us streamline the loan process for those with complex credit histories, enabling us to assist more clients in achieving their dreams of homeownership.

Moreover, our active presence in the community further solidified our commitment to empowering and uplifting individuals and families, regardless of their financial past.

Embracing the power of community events was undoubtedly a game-changer for our business, allowing us to make a tangible difference in people's lives while elevating our brand as a trusted, reliable, and compassionate lending partner.

When the mortgage industry faced a catastrophic crash in 2008, I recognized the need to adapt and pivot to stay relevant and successful. With this in mind, I founded a business consulting company aimed at helping small business owners establish a solid foundation for sustainable growth.

While I had initially hoped to incorporate live events into my strategies, the timing didn't align with the market's needs at that time.

Despite the challenges, I remained dedicated to supporting small businesses through various avenues. I focused on developing innovative solutions and providing expert guidance to guide entrepreneurs in navigating the turbulent economic landscape.

My passion for live events and the transformative power they hold never waned, though it took a back seat as I explored other lead generation and business building methods.

As the economy began to recover and businesses regained their footing, I noticed a resurgence of interest in live events. This observation presented the perfect opportunity to reintegrate event-based strategies into my consulting services. I knew that these experiences could foster meaningful connections, enhance brand visibility, and contribute to the success of the small businesses I served.

By combining my expertise in business consulting with my passion for live events, I was able to provide a unique and practical approach to business growth. Which allowed me to help countless small businesses thrive in the face of adversity and build a strong foundation for a brighter, more prosperous future.

However, it wasn't until after the COVID-19 pandemic had ended, that I had the chance to plan large-scale live events again, this time for small businesses. This opportunity reignited my passion for helping small business owners harness the potential of live events. I realized the significant impact a well-planned and executed event could have on a small business's growth and success, which motivated me to create the Bankable Events, LLC brand.

With a renewed sense of purpose and determination, I set out to help small businesses harness the potential of live events and experience the same level of triumph. Drawing upon my extensive business development and event planning background, I aim to empower small business owners with the knowledge and tools to create unforgettable experiences.

With over 20 years of invaluable experience spanning corporate event planning and nearly 20 years of entrepreneurship, I am uniquely positioned to share my expertise in a comprehensive guide tailored specifically for small business owners. This guide will enable you to harness the transformative power of live events, opening up new avenues for growth, collaboration, and success.

In this book, I will share my insights and fundamental strategies for creating successful events, from the initial planning stages to executing a seamless event that leaves a lasting impression on attendees. Whether you've hosted events in the past or you're toying with the idea of hosting your first live event, this book will provide you with the tools and techniques you need to build your brand, drive revenue, and grow a sustainable business through the power of live events.

Understanding the Benefits of Hosting an Event for Your Business

Hosting a live event for your business can be a powerful tool for growth and success. Whether you're a small business owner looking to increase brand awareness, generate leads, or build relationships with your community, hosting a live event can provide various benefits to help you achieve your goals. This chapter will explore the primary benefits of hosting a live event for your business and why you should think about adding this powerful strategy to your marketing mix.

Increased Brand Awareness:

Hosting live events increases brand awareness and exposure for your business. You can showcase your brand, products, and services to a broader audience by bringing people together in unique and memorable ways. Increased brand awareness can bolster your reputation as a thought leader and increase your brand's visibility like no other method.

Lead Generation:

Hosting a live event is a great way to generate leads and build your customer base. Creating an interactive and engaging experience can attract new customers and build relationships. Connecting with quality leads is especially beneficial for small business owners looking to grow your business quickly.

Community Building:

Hosting an event can help you build relationships inside of your community. By bringing people together in fun and engaging ways, you can build a sense of community around your brand and create opportunities for your customers to connect. A strong sense of belonging can increase loyalty and strengthen your customer base.

Revenue Generation:

Hosting an event is an excellent way to generate revenue for your business. Whether you charge admission or offer sponsorships, hosting an event can provide a new source of income that can help you scale your business and achieve your financial goals.

Mastering the art of monetizing your events is an area in which we excel. We can help you generate revenue during and after your event with many innovative strategies. We can teach you how to maximize your earnings while simultaneously providing exceptional value to your clients, creating a winning formula for sustained success.

Networking Opportunities:

Hosting an event can provide valuable networking opportunities for your business. You can connect with other business owners, entrepreneurs, and industry leaders by bringing people together in a relaxed and informal setting. Well-thought-out networking events build valuable relationships and provide an opportunity to make new connections and collaborations.

Building Relationships:

Hosting an event provides an excellent opportunity to build relationships with your customers, partners, and other stakeholders. You can connect with them personally and meaningfully in order to establish long-lasting relationships leading to future business opportunities. Cultivating relationships within your community takes the guesswork out of knowing what your customers want so you can customize your offerings to meet their needs.

Improving Employee Morale:

Hosting a live event can have a positive influence on your employees. It can provide fun and engaging opportunities to connect and build stronger relationships. Increased engagement can improve morale and motivation, which can have many positive effects on your business.

Positioning Your Business as a Thought Leader:

Hosting a well-planned and executed event can position your business as a thought leader. Events provide a platform to showcase your expertise and demonstrate your commitment to innovation and excellence. Positioning yourself well will help you stand out and attract new customers and power partners.

Hosting live events for your business has the potential to provide many benefits to help you achieve your business goals. Whether you want to increase brand awareness, generate leads, build relationships with your community, or generate revenue, hosting events is a powerful tool for success. In the next chapter, we'll explore how you can secure sponsors or partners to help underwrite the costs of your next event.

As you progress through this book, think about your "why" and what you hope to accomplish by hosting a live event. A big part of planning is beginning with the end in mind.

What results are you looking for?

Sponsorship and Partnerships: How to Get Help Paying for Your Event

Sponsorship and partnerships are valuable ways to offset the costs of hosting an event for your business. Whether you are planning a small workshop or a large-scale conference, these relationships provide a crucial source of funding and support.

To attract sponsors and partners, you must communicate the value they receive from being involved with your event. Sponsorship may include exposure to a new audience, the opportunity to showcase their products or services, or build brand awareness and credibility.

Once you determine the value that sponsors and partners will receive at your event, it's time to start developing a sponsorship strategy. Initial steps include creating a sponsorship pitch deck or package outlining the benefits of partnering with your event that include the different sponsorship levels available.

Your presentation must be professional, clear, and concise when contacting potential sponsors and partners. Explain your event's value to their business and what specific benefits they can expect from their investment. Be prepared to answer any questions and provide additional information as needed.

Another critical aspect of attracting sponsors and partners is to have a well-defined target audience. Understanding the demographics and interests of your attendees can help you identify potential sponsors and partners that would be a good fit for your event.

It's essential to be flexible and open to negotiation. Sponsorship and partnership arrangements can take many forms. Be willing to employ creative options to reach a mutually beneficial agreement.

Let's delve into crafting a successful sponsorship and partnership strategy. We will explore the most effective methods to engage with potential sponsors and partners, as well as discuss the art of negotiation and finalizing mutually beneficial agreements. With the right approach and a clear understanding of your event's value, you can secure the funding and support you need to host a successful and influential event.

Creating a Successful Sponsorship and Partnership Strategy:

osting successful and profitable events is easier with the support of sponsors and partners. These partnerships provide financial support and additional resources to help make your event a success. However, reaching out to potential sponsors and partners and negotiating the terms of these agreements can be challenging and, at times, intimidating.

To create a successful sponsorship and partnership strategy, you need to understand your target audience and the goals you want to achieve by hosting your event. Once you have clarity, you can start researching potential sponsors and partners and developing a plan to reach out to them.

Identify Your Target Market: Before reaching out to potential sponsors and partners, you need to understand your target audience.

- Who is your event for?
- What are their interests and needs?
- What type of businesses would be a good fit for your event and your audience?
- What problem are you solving?

- Why are you qualified?

Understanding your target market will help you determine the types of sponsors and partners you should be targeting.

Determine Your Sponsorship Packages: Once you clearly understand your target market, the next step is to determine your sponsorship packages.

- What types of sponsorships do you want to offer?

- Will you provide monetary sponsorships, product sponsorships, or a combination of both?

- What benefits will you offer to your sponsors and partners?

Identify Potential Sponsors and Partners: Once you have determined your sponsorship packages, it's time to research and identify companies and organizations that would be a good fit for your event. Look for companies that align with your brand and target audience and have a history of supporting similar events. Connecting with potential sponsors can be done through various methods, including online research, networking, and word of mouth.

For example, if you organize a health and wellness conference, a natural fit for a sponsor might be a prominent fitness brand, a health food company, or a renowned wellness center. By partnering with a sponsor whose offerings resonate with your target audience, you can create a synergistic relationship that benefits both parties and enhances the event experience.

Reach Out to Potential Sponsors and Partners: Once you have identified your potential sponsors and partners, contact them so you can personalize and tailor your presentation to align with their goals. You can do this through email, phone, or in-person meetings. When reaching out, clearly explain the benefits of sponsoring or partnering with your event and why it is a good fit for their business.

There are many reasons to tailor your sponsorship presentations to individual companies. First and foremost, it demonstrates that you've taken the time to research and understand the company's values, goals, and target audience, which reflects your genuine interest in forming a partnership. This targeted approach effectively addresses the company's unique needs and objectives, emphasizing the specific benefits and opportunities your event offers.

Furthermore, personalizing your presentation helps build rapport. It fosters a sense of connection between your event and the prospective sponsor, creating a powerful emotional engagement that can motivate them to collaborate with you. A well-researched and customized presentation showcases your professionalism and commitment to creating a mutually beneficial partnership, boosting your credibility in the eyes of the potential sponsor.

By addressing individual companies' specific interests and concerns, tailored sponsorship presentations are more likely to resonate and lead to successful partnerships, improving your conversion rates and event success.

Negotiate and Finalize Agreements: During the negotiation and finalization of agreements, you must be transparent about your objectives and what you intend to accomplish through the partnership.

Additionally, consider the benefits and value the potential sponsor will gain from collaborating with you. Strive to establish a mutually beneficial relationship where both parties experience a positive outcome.

Be open about what you can offer and what you expect in return, and be willing to compromise when it makes sense. Compromising demonstrates your commitment to forming a long-lasting and successful partnership, which can help strengthen the relationship and encourage future collaborations.

Stay adaptable and receptive to diverse partnership opportunities. Sponsors and partners may have their own objectives and interests, and being open to different types of agreements can help you find a mutually beneficial solution.

Negotiation flexibility often leads to more creative and innovative solutions, enabling you to adapt your proposal to better align with the sponsor's goals and objectives and enhance the partnership's success.

Protect yourself and your relationships. When finalizing agreements, put everything in writing to avoid misunderstandings and confirm everyone is clear on the terms of the deal.

Creating a successful sponsorship and partnership strategy is integral to hosting a successful event. By researching potential sponsors and partners, personalizing your outreach, and negotiating and finalizing agreements effectively, you can secure the support you need to make your event successful.

Make a list of five people and companies you know who would make great sponsors for your next event.

Identify Your Target Audience and Event Goals

One of the most crucial components of planning a successful event is identifying your target audience and event goals. Creating a "persona" or "avatar" involves understanding your ideal attendees, what they want and need from the event, and how to best fulfill those needs. Knowing your target audience and event goals empowers you to customize your event content to their preferences.

There are several steps involved in identifying your target audience and event goals:

Before you start planning your live event, it is critical to identify and understand your target audience. This information will help guide your event planning decisions, from selecting the right venue and date to choosing the content you will present and the activities you will include. Your target audience will also help you determine the best event style, from a small, intimate retreat to a large-scale conference.

Before getting started you must let go of the myth that "everyone" is your target market. Defining your target audience seems like a daunting task. Still, with the right tools and techniques, you can quickly identify the people most likely to be interested in your event.

The first step is to determine the purpose of your event. What is the main goal you are trying to achieve? Is it to educate people about a particular topic, generate business leads, or build relationships with existing customers? Do you want to entertain your attendees or honor them with an award?

Once you clearly understand your event's purpose, you can start to identify your target audience. Here are some steps you can take to define your target audience:

Analyze your existing customer base: If you already have one, start by analyzing their demographics, such as age, gender, location, and interests. This information can help determine the people most likely to attend your event.

Conduct market research: Market research can provide valuable insights into your target audience. Ask people you know, conduct online surveys, put together focus groups, or perform customer interviews to gather information about the people most likely to attend your event.

Look at your competitors: Analyze the events your competitors host and the types of people they attract. This information will help you determine what kind of people enjoy attending events and what style of events most appeal to them.

Use social media: Social media can be valuable for identifying your target audience. Use tools like Twitter, Facebook, or LinkedIn to find people interested in the topics you will cover at your event. You can use social media to connect with potential attendees and get feedback on your event ideas.

Once you understand your target audience, use this information to produce a successful event that meets their needs and expectations. Your target audience determines the right venue, date, content, and activities for your event, ensuring it is a memorable and impactful experience for everyone.

Next, determine their pain points, frustrations, and fears:

When planning a live event, it's essential to understand your target audience's pain points, frustrations, and fears. Doing so can create an event that speaks to these issues and meaningfully provides real value to your attendees.

Dialing in your ideal attendees' demographic, geographic, and psychographic characteristics will help you outline this information. Surveys, focus groups, and customer interviews are valuable information-gathering tools.

Get clear on the pain points, struggles, and fears as the challenges and sources of discontent your target audience faces daily. These obstacles act as major barriers preventing them from achieving their desired objectives. These can range from practical issues, such as:

Lack of confidence: Your attendees might grapple with self-doubt and insecurity, which can be sizable roadblocks. These emotional hurdles may hinder them from making critical decisions or taking decisive action, whether in their personal lives or professional endeavors. By addressing and offering solutions to overcome such challenges, you can empower your audience to break free from these constraints and unlock their full potential.

Fear of failure: The fear of failure can be a double-edged sword. At the same time, it can serve as a powerful motivator or become an obstacle to succeed. Your target audience may need to be aware of their apprehension towards taking risks, making mistakes, or potentially losing money. This fear can stifle their creativity, hinder their growth, and prevent them from seizing opportunities that could lead to meaningful advancements in their personal or professional lives. By addressing these concerns and offering strategies to help them overcome their fears, you can empower your audience to embrace challenges and unlock their true potential, paving the way for a more fulfilling and prosperous future.

Overwhelm: Your ideal clients might feel overwhelmed due to the extensive array of tasks and responsibilities they must juggle. This constant sense of pressure can lead to burnout, decreased productivity, and diminished overall well-being.

By addressing these challenges and offering practical solutions, such as time management techniques, prioritization strategies, and self-care practices, you can help your audience regain control over their workload and achieve a more balanced, fulfilling, and efficient approach to managing their personal and professional lives.

Burnout: The stress and pressure that come with everyday life can accumulate over time and eventually result in burnout. Burnout is a complete physical, emotional, and mental exhaustion that can harm an individual's well-being and quality of life.

This overwhelming exhaustion can manifest in various ways, such as reduced motivation, diminished productivity, increased irritability, and even health issues.

By addressing the factors contributing to burnout and offering stress management, self-care, and work-life balance strategies, you can help your audience overcome this debilitating condition and regain their vitality, enthusiasm, and ability to thrive personally and professionally.

Isolation: Your ideal client might experience feelings of isolation from their family, peers, or employees, which can impede their ability to collaborate effectively and make well-informed decisions. This disconnection can stem from long working hours, communication barriers, or a lack of social support. This isolation can hinder their personal and professional growth and negatively affect their emotional well-being.

By addressing these feelings of isolation and offering solutions to foster better connections, such as improving communication skills, building a supportive network, and promoting a healthy work-life balance, you can help your audience reestablish meaningful relationships with those around them. This renewed sense of connection can enhance their collaborative abilities, decision-making skills, and satisfaction in their personal and professional lives.

Financial stress: Financial stress is a prevalent issue in today's economy, affecting various individuals across various walks of life. Economic uncertainty, mounting debts, and increasing living expenses can contribute to anxiety and worry about one's financial well-being. This stress can substantially impact an individual's physical and mental health, relationships, and quality of life.

By addressing the issue of financial stress and offering practical solutions, such as budgeting strategies, debt management techniques, and income diversification, you can help your audience regain control over their financial situation. Empowering them with the tools and knowledge to manage their finances effectively can alleviate their stress, enhance their sense of security, and improve their well-being and satisfaction with life.

Once you pinpoint your target audience's pain points, struggles, and fears, you can use this valuable insight to craft an event that delivers genuine value and resonates with attendees. By structuring your event's breakout sessions, panel discussions, and offerings around the topics most relevant to your audience, you can create a tailored experience that addresses their needs and concerns.

This targeted approach guarantees that your event content is engaging and informative, providing your audience with practical solutions and strategies they can implement. By directly addressing their challenges and offering actionable steps for improvement, your event will leave a lasting impression, helping your attendees overcome hurdles and achieve their goals in both their personal and professional lives.

Your attendees' preferences:

Examine your target audience's event format, content, and location preferences. For example, do they prefer a more traditional conference format or a more interactive workshop format? Do they like keynote speeches or panel discussions?

To gather this information, you can use surveys and questionnaires. Before your event, send out surveys and questionnaires to collect information about food and beverage choices, preferred activities, and interests.

Social media is an excellent way to engage with your attendees and ask questions about their preferences, the topics they are most interested in, and what they expect from your event.

If you have held events in the past, analyze the data you have collected from previous attendees to understand your potential attendees' preferences and what they enjoyed about previous events.

Don't get caught up in emotion or your preferences. Remember, this event is about meeting the needs of your attendees. The more clarity you have, the easier it will be to get people to attend your events.

Now that you know who you want to serve, it's time to figure out how to design an event that speaks to their situation. Creating goals for your event will make certain that you create the type of content required to exceed their expectations.

Set specific event goals:

When setting event goals, keep your attendees' expectations and business goals in mind.

Goals might include being mindful about:

Attendee Expectations:

Meeting attendees' expectations at an event is critical because it helps build their trust and credibility. Attendees come to your event with a certain set of expectations. It is crucial to meet or exceed their expectations to avoid disappointment or a negative perception of your brand.

By understanding your attendees' needs and preferences, you can create an experience that increases customer satisfaction, improves brand loyalty, and future referrals.

Business Objectives:

Aligning your event goals with your attendees' expectations ensures that your event successfully achieves its desired outcomes. Whether your plan generates leads, increases sales, or builds brand awareness, clearly understanding your attendees' needs and expectations can help create a more effective and transformational event.

There are many possible business objectives for hosting a live event. Some of the most common ones include:

Increasing brand awareness:

Hosting a live event is a powerful tool to increase brand awareness and gain exposure for your business. Here are a few ways to achieve this:

Offer Unique Content:

To stand out and truly make an impression, you must provide unique content highlighting your brand's products, services, and expertise. By offering valuable insights, innovative ideas, and actionable solutions, you can showcase your brand's knowledge and skills and position yourself and your business as a thought leader.

This approach enhances your brand's credibility and reputation and encourages trust and loyalty among your target audience. As you share your expertise and demonstrate a genuine interest in helping your attendees overcome their challenges, they will be more inclined to engage with your brand and seek out your products or services in the future.

By consistently offering valuable and distinctive content, your brand can become synonymous with industry-leading expertise, fostering long-lasting connections with your audience and solidifying your position as a go-to resource.

Create a Memorable Experience:

Creating a memorable event that offers attendees a unique and enjoyable experience is crucial to leaving a lasting impression, enhancing brand recognition, and setting your business apart from the competition. To achieve this, focus on delivering exceptional content, engaging presentations, and interactive elements that resonate with your audience and cater to their unique needs and interests.

Moreover, it would be best to incorporate creative elements like immersive environments, captivating visuals, or experiential activities to offer attendees an unforgettable experience. These distinctive features make your event more enjoyable and help forge a strong emotional connection with your brand.

By offering an unparalleled event experience, you'll create positive associations with your brand, encouraging attendees to share their experiences with others and fostering brand loyalty. Creating exceptional event experiences distinguishes your business in a crowded marketplace and solidifies your reputation as a leader in your industry.

Utilize Social Media: Leveraging social media to promote your event and encouraging attendees to share their experiences on their channels can enhance your reach and boost brand awareness. By utilizing various platforms, such as Facebook, Twitter, Instagram, and LinkedIn, you can create buzz around your event, engage with your target audience, and provide updates and teasers leading up to the big day.

In addition to your promotional efforts, empowering attendees to become brand ambassadors by sharing their event experiences on social media can amplify your message. Please encourage them to use a dedicated event hashtag, post photos and videos, and interact with your brand's accounts. This attendee-generated content (AGC) not only provides social proof of the value and enjoyment of your event but helps reach a wider audience who may have already been aware of your brand or event.

By actively promoting your event on social media and harnessing the power of AGC, you can create a ripple effect that extends your reach, raises brand awareness, and ultimately contributes to the success of your event and business.

Networking Opportunities: Facilitating networking opportunities for attendees with each other and with your business is essential for fostering connections and establishing your brand as a central hub for industry professionals. You can create an environment where meaningful relationships can be forged and ideas exchanged by providing dedicated spaces, activities, or sessions encouraging interaction and collaboration.

These networking opportunities enhance the event experience and contribute to the attendees' professional growth, as they can connect with potential partners, clients, or mentors. This added value reflects positively on your brand, as participants will associate your business with the connections and opportunities they have gained.

Furthermore, by actively engaging with attendees during these networking sessions, your business can strengthen its relationships with potential customers, partners, and influencers. This direct engagement helps solidify your brand's position in the attendees' minds, creating a lasting impression and increasing the likelihood of future collaborations and partnerships.

By offering plenty of networking opportunities at your event, you can position your brand as a significant player in your industry while promoting a sense of community and connection that creates a lasting impression on attendees.

Leverage Sponsorships and Partnerships: Collaborating with other businesses to co-host events or securing sponsors interested in supporting your event can increase your brand's visibility and reach. You can tap into new networks and expand your event's promotional efforts by forming strategic partnerships with companies that share a similar target audience or complement your brand's offerings.

Co-hosting events allows businesses to leverage their unique strengths, resources, and contacts to create an even more impactful experience for attendees. These types of collaborations often lead to more comprehensive and diverse event programs, enhancing the value for participants and creating opportunities for cross-promotion and audience growth.

Securing event sponsors can provide additional resources and credibility, enabling you to enhance the event experience. Sponsors can offer financial support, in-kind contributions, or expertise, which can contribute to the event's success and help attract a larger audience.

By partnering with other businesses or securing sponsors for your event, you can amplify your brand's visibility, expand your reach, and create a more compelling and engaging experience for attendees, which will contribute to your brand's growth and success within your industry.

Driving sales:

Driving sales at your event can be achieved through various strategies. Some of these strategies include:

→ **Offering special deals or promotions:**

Providing exclusive discounts or special deals to your attendees during the event can be a powerful incentive for them to purchase on the spot. These limited-time offers create a sense of urgency and exclusivity, enticing attendees to take advantage of the savings and unique opportunities available only to event participants.

→ By offering these special deals, you can demonstrate the value of attending your event and create a positive association with your brand leading to increased sales and revenue and fostering customer loyalty among those who benefit from the exclusive offers.

→ In addition to driving on-site sales, these special deals can serve as a talking point and promotional tool for your event. Attendees may share the details of the exclusive offers with their networks, further spreading the word about your event and brand and potentially attracting more customers and future attendees.

Providing product demonstrations:

Live demonstrations or product samples at your event effectively showcase your products or services and help attendees understand the value of what you're offering. Live demonstrations allow attendees to see your products or services in action. In contrast, product samples provide a tangible experience and a way to test and experience your offerings first-hand.

These demonstrations and samples can differentiate your brand from competitors and establish your products or services as unique and valuable. By providing an interactive and engaging experience, you can leave a lasting impression on attendees, prompting them to purchase your products or services and recommend them to others.

These live demonstrations and product samples can serve as a promotional tool for your brand, creating buzz around your products or services and encouraging attendees to share their experiences with others. By leveraging the power of social media and word-of-mouth marketing, you can extend your brand's reach and attract new customers beyond the event.

Launching a new product or service:

Making your product launch memorable is crucial to stimulating interest and generating excitement around your brand and new offering. You can captivate your audience and create a lasting impression by incorporating elements such as a product reveal, celebrity endorsements, or other enticing features.

A product reveal can generate a sense of anticipation and intrigue, encouraging attendees to engage with your brand and learn more about the new offering. You can achieve this by creating a dramatic unveiling or teaser campaign leading to the launch. Product reveals generate excitement and anticipation among your target audience.

Celebrity endorsements can lend credibility and prestige to your brand and new product, particularly if the celebrity has a significant following or influence within your target market. Their endorsement can help amplify your message and create a positive association with your brand, leading to increased sales and customer loyalty.

Other exciting elements, such as interactive displays, live performances, or immersive experiences, can add a unique and memorable aspect to your launch, creating a positive and lasting impression on attendees. These elements allow attendees to engage with your brand and new product, fostering a deeper connection and interest.

→ **Creating a sense of urgency:**

Using limited-time offers or early bird discounts is a proven strategy to create a sense of urgency and encourage attendees to take advantage of the opportunity to purchase. These promotions are particularly effective when exclusive to event attendees, creating a perception of added value for those who attend.

Providing time-sensitive or early bird discounts creates a sense of urgency and scarcity, motivating attendees to take immediate action and purchase. This tactic is particularly effective when the offers are sizable or only available for a limited time.

These promotions can incentivize attendees to purchase the spot rather than waiting and potentially losing interest or forgetting about your offering resulting in increased sales and revenue for your business.

Early bird discounts are an effective way to reward attendees who register or purchase tickets early, encouraging them to commit to attending your event and creating a buzz around it. This strategy can help you gauge attendance and plan accordingly.

→ **Making it easy to buy:**

A smooth and hassle-free purchasing process increases attendees' follow through on their intention to buy your products or services. You can achieve this by offering multiple payment options and organizing a well-structured checkout process.

By providing various payment options such as credit cards, PayPal, or mobile payments, attendees can choose the payment method that is the most convenient for them. This helps to reduce the probability of abandoned transactions or lost sales resulting from limited payment options. Additionally, an effortless checkout experience can improve attendee satisfaction and increase the prospect of repeat business.

A well-organized checkout process can reduce frustration and confusion for attendees. To achieve this, clearly indicate the cost of the product or service, provide a detailed breakdown of any fees or taxes, and offer a seamless and secure checkout experience.

Make your customer support team available to answer any questions or concerns attendees may have during purchasing. Providing excellent customer service builds trust and confidence in your brand. It provides attendees with a positive experience from start to finish.

If you sell high-ticket services, consider using a lending partner to handle the financing. Breaking up large purchases into smaller payments has been known to increase conversions. PayPal now offers a buy now, pay later option for those who qualify.

→ **Providing follow-up materials:**

Providing attendees with follow-up materials, such as brochures or product catalogs, is an effective way to remind them of the products or services they saw at the event and encourage them to purchase after the event. These materials can be a reference for attendees who want to learn more about your brand or products.

By providing follow-up materials, you are extending the reach and outcome of your event beyond the day of the event. Attendees can review the materials at their leisure and share them with their colleagues, friends, or family, helping to increase brand awareness.

Furthermore, these materials can provide additional information and insights that attendees may have yet to have the opportunity to see or learn about during the event itself. They can showcase the unique features and benefits of your products or services and provide a clear call to action (CTA) for attendees to make a purchase.

Follow-up materials should be well-designed, easy to read, and provide value to the attendees. These materials can include tips on accessing or using your products or services, requests for customer testimonials, or promotional offers to incentivize additional purchases.

→ **Gaining insights and feedback:**

Hosting a live event provides a unique opportunity to interact directly with your target audience and gain valuable insights into their needs, preferences, and opinions. You can collect feedback through various means, such as surveys, focus groups, and one-on-one conversations with attendees.

By gathering feedback from attendees, you can gain insights into the pain points and struggles which can help inform the development of new products or services that address these needs. You can also gather feedback on existing products or services, allowing you to make improvements or adjustments based on their feedback.

Hosting a live event creates the opportunity for you to build relationships with your target audience and establish your brand as a thought leader and trusted resource in your industry. Nurturing relationships inside your community can lead to increased customer loyalty, advocacy, and positive word-of-mouth marketing.

By analyzing attendance, engagement, and other metrics, you can better understand what resonates with your audience and what aspects of your event were most impactful. You can then use this information to formulate future events and marketing strategies.

→ **Improving customer engagement:**

Improving customer engagement at a live event is crucial to building relationships with attendees and creating a positive and memorable experience. One way to do this is by creating interactive and immersive experiences that allow attendees to engage with your brand and each other.

Roundtable discussions, cocktail receptions, and networking exercises are just a few examples of interactive experiences that can create a sense of community and encourage attendees to participate and engage with your brand. These activities allow attendees to learn from each other, share their experiences and insights, and connect with like-minded individuals.

By creating interactive and immersive experiences and encouraging social media engagement, you are improving customer engagement and creating an environment that fosters a positive and memorable experience for attendees. A well thought-out event agenda has the potential to contribute to increased customer loyalty, advocacy, and, most importantly, a positive result on your business's bottom line.

→ **Demonstrating your expertise:**

Establishing your brand as a thought leader in your industry is a fundamental element to building trust with your target audience. One of the most effective ways to achieve this is by demonstrating your expertise through various public speaking engagements.

Giving a keynote presentation, conducting a training work-shop, or participating in a panel discussion are all excellent ways to showcase your knowledge and expertise. These engagements allow you to share your insights and perspective on industry trends and challenges, positioning your brand as a go-to resource for information and guidance.

Keynote presentations allow you to deliver compelling and informative talks on specific topics related to your industry. Speaking is the number one way to position your brand as a thought leader and build credibility and trust with your audience.

Training workshops provide attendees practical skills and knowledge to apply to their businesses or work. Sharing valuable information demonstrates your expertise while delivering tangible value to your audience.

Participating in a panel discussion allows you to dialogue with other industry experts and share your perspectives and insights with a broader audience. Surrounding yourself with like-minded leaders provides a platform to showcase your expertise and build relationships with other thought leaders in your industry.

→ **Building community:**

Building a community with potential clients is essential to establishing a solid brand and increasing customer loyalty. Hosting a live event provides a unique opportunity to create a welcoming and inclusive atmosphere where attendees can connect, develop new relationships, and build a sense of belonging.

One way to create this sense of community is by designing the event that encourages networking and interaction among attendees. This can include interactive activities, icebreaker exercises, and designated areas for attendees to connect and network with each other.

Involving local organizations, businesses, or community groups in your event planning and execution is another effective way to build community. By partnering with other organizations, you can expand your reach and establish strong partnerships that benefit your business and the community.

Hosting events that benefit local organizations or causes can strengthen relationships between your business and the community. Community events can include charity fundraisers, volunteer events, or other initiatives that give back to the local community.

→ **Monetizing your brand**:

When it comes to monetizing your live event, set realistic goals that align with the nature of your event, your target audience, and the resources you have available to you. Your strategy should take into account the size of your event, the demographic of your target audience, and the costs associated with hosting the event.

To generate revenue from a live event, ticket sales are one of the most popular methods. Set a reasonable price for the tickets that accurately reflects the value that attendees will receive from the event. Depending on the nature of your event, it might be beneficial to offer tiered pricing options to accommodate different budgets.

In addition to ticket sales, you can monetize your event by selling products or services related to your brand. An event pop-up store can offer a wide range of products or services, such as merchandise, digital products, or consulting services. Verify that your offerings are relevant to your audience and provide tangible value.

Sponsorships and partnerships are another effective way to monetize your event. You can increase your reach and access new audiences by partnering with other brands or businesses. (Grab your FREE Sponsorship Pitch Deck from the resource section at the end of the book.)

→ **Budgeting:**

Budgeting is a critical aspect of event planning and can affect the success and profitability of your event.

You will need to set aside money for your event venue. Your budget should include rental fees, insurance, and permits or licenses. The venue you choose will contribute a significant percentage to the total cost of your event, so take a close look at your options and select a venue that fits your budget.

Presume you're providing meals at your event. In that case, your event budget must include food and beverage (F&B), which consists of the cost of food and beverages and any catering fees, service charges, gratuities, and tax. Depending on the nature of your event, you may need additional amenities such as bar service or specialty food stations.

AV (audio-visual) costs routinely include equipment like projectors, sound systems, lighting, and staging. Depending on the complexity of your event, you may need to hire AV professionals to manage and operate this equipment.

Marketing and promotion are other key expensess when planning a live event. These costs include social media advertising, print materials, and email campaigns. Think carefully about your marketing strategy to make sure you effectively reach your target audience within your budget.

Lastly, staffing costs include but may not be limited to event coordinators, assistants, security personnel, and other staff to manage and execute your event successfully.

Hosting a live event can help achieve various business objectives, and these are just a few examples.

The specific goals you set for your event will depend on your unique business needs and objectives. Identify these goals so you can make informed decision-making throughout the event planning process, guiding choices around content, format, and location.

As you plan your event, understanding your business objectives will be invaluable. It will guide you in designing an event tailored to your target audience's needs and interests while effectively aligning with your overall business strategy.

In the next chapter, we will explore the importance of event themes and how to choose a suitable theme for your event. A well-chosen theme will elevate the attendee experience, create a memorable event, and reinforce your brand message.

Creating a Theme: Finding the Heart of Your Event

$\mathcal{S}$etting a theme for your event is essential to the planning process. You should directly tie the theme to the problem or challenge you are trying to solve for your attendees. By choosing a theme that aligns with your event goals and the needs of your target audience, you can create a more cohesive and impactful event.

To set a theme for your event:

1. Start by identifying the problem you are trying to solve or the challenge you want to address.

2. Once you have a theme in mind, decide how to incorporate it into every aspect of the event, from the decor and branding to the content and activities.

3. Reflect your event theme in your marketing materials and communications so that attendees understand why they are attending your event and what they can expect to experience.

Throughout my event planning career, I have planned hundreds of themed events. Themes help entice potential attendees to register and leave a lasting impression after the event. Well-thought-out themes breathe life into the event and are relevant to each facet of the planning stage.

I have found that most themes will fit into one of these categories:

Innovative Solutions - The innovation theme is an excellent choice for businesses highlighting their expertise in cutting-edge products or services within their industry. This theme is about showcasing the latest advancements and solutions, which attract attendees eager to learn about the newest and most innovative products or services.

By choosing an innovation theme for your event, you can position your business as a thought leader in your industry who is always on the cutting edge of innovation. A unique theme can create a sense of excitement and anticipation among attendees who are eager to learn from your business and see what new ideas you have to offer.

One of the key benefits of the innovation theme is that it allows you to focus on the unique features and benefits of your products or services. By highlighting your innovative aspects, you can help attendees better understand how your solutions solve their problems and meet their needs.

The innovation theme is an excellent choice for businesses looking to showcase their expertise and position themselves as leaders in their industry. By leveraging this theme effectively, you can create an informative and engaging event, leaving a lasting impression on attendees and driving growth and success for your business.

Networking and Collaboration - The networking and collaboration theme is an excellent choice for businesses that want to create a space for professionals from different industries to connect, build relationships, and collaborate. By choosing this theme, you can establish your business as a hub for industry professionals, which will increase your brand visibility and reputation.

One of the key benefits of the networking and collaboration theme is that it provides attendees with the opportunity to connect with others who have similar interests or needs. This can foster a sense of community and create a supportive environment where attendees can learn from each other, share ideas, and build relationships.

Additionally, bringing together professionals from different industries creates a space to cross-pollinate ideas and innovation. It is well-known that networking can lead to new business opportunities and partnerships that can help drive your business's growth and success.

By hosting an event focusing on connecting industry professionals, you can showcase your expertise and knowledge and establish your business as a leader in your field.

Education and Empowerment - The education and training theme is the perfect choice for businesses that want to provide attendees with valuable knowledge, tools, certifications, and resources to support their success in their professional or personal lives. By focusing on education and training, you can establish your business as an authority in your niche, build a loyal following, and provide attendees with tangible benefits.

One of the key benefits of the education and training theme is that it allows you to provide attendees with the knowledge and skills they need to achieve their goals. You can set up educational events in various ways, including training workshops, keynote speeches, or certification programs that teach attendees new skills, strategies, and best practices. By providing value, you can help attendees feel more confident and empowered personally or professionally.

By providing attendees with valuable information and insights, you can establish your business as a trusted source of knowledge and expertise. Being known as a trusted expert builds trust and credibility with your audience, which can lead to increased sales and growth for your business.

Another benefit of the education and training theme is that it creates a sense of community among attendees. Bringing together people with a common interest or goal can create a supportive environment where attendees can connect, share ideas, and build relationships.

Fun and Adventure - The entertainment and fun theme is an obvious choice for businesses that want to create a memorable experience for attendees and build a lighthearted and fun atmosphere. By focusing on entertainment and fun, you can design an enjoyable and engaging event for attendees and associate your business with positive emotions.

One of the key benefits of the entertainment and fun theme is that it builds a sense of excitement and anticipation among attendees. You can create a fun and memorable atmosphere by providing engaging and entertaining activities, such as live music, games, or interactive experiences. Entertainment-based themes build buzz around your event and can increase attendance, as attendees are more likely to share their positive experiences with others.

The entertainment and fun theme effectively creates a sense of community and builds relationships among attendees. By providing opportunities for attendees to connect and engage with each other through team-building activities or interactive games, you establish a sense of camaraderie and build lasting relationships among attendees.

Furthermore, by creating an enjoyable and entertaining atmosphere, you establish your business as a brand that values fun and creativity. Hosting a unique event attracts new customers and increases customer loyalty, as attendees are more likely to associate your business with positive emotions and experiences.

Making a Difference - The social or environmental cause theme is an intelligent choice for conscious mission-driven businesses that want to demonstrate their commitment to social or environmental causes. Incorporating a reason into your event can attract attendees who share your values and build a loyal following.

One of the key benefits of the social or environmental cause theme is that it aligns your business with a larger purpose. By showcasing your commitment to a social or environmental cause, you establish your business as a brand that values sustainability, responsibility, and making a difference. Conscious events attract customers who are passionate about these causes and build a loyal following of like-minded individuals.

The social or environmental cause theme efficiently builds community and fosters relationships among attendees. Bringing together individuals with a common cause can create camaraderie and build lasting relationships among attendees. Attendees with a mission-based mindset want to bring about transformation even after the event itself and attendees are more likely to continue to work together and support each other in their shared mission.

Incorporating a cause into your event can drive awareness and support the cause itself. It can even create a ripple effect on the community demonstrating your business's commitment to creating positive change.

Ultimately, your theme should reflect your brand, values, and the solutions you offer, while addressing the needs of your target audience. You can create a memorable and impactful event by authentically tying your theme to the problem you are solving for your attendees.

You might think that's all fine and good, but how does that help me fill my event with people?

Developing a value proposition and "big" promise for your event is crucial to attracting and retaining attendees. It sets the stage for why your event is relevant, meaningful, and valuable to your target audience.

It would be best if you closely tied your value proposition and big promise to your event theme, so they can work together to tackle your target audience's most pressing problems and pain points.

To develop your value proposition and "big" promise, clearly define your target audience and their most pressing problems. Your "big" promise will help solve challenges related to their personal or professional life, such as lack of time, knowledge, or resources. Once you understand your target audience's pain points, think about how they can solve those problems by attending your event.

Next, craft a clear and concise value proposition that outlines what attendees will receive from your event. Your value proposition will include specific outcomes, such as increased knowledge, new skills, or connections with other attendees. Your value proposition should highlight what makes your event unique and different from others in your industry.

Be sure to determine what makes your event unique from others in the market. In simple terms, avoid using industry jargon, and outline the value you offer that your competitors don't. Use language that is clear, concise, and easily understood. For this exercise, you need to use the KISS method!

Emphasize the results your attendees will experience by attending your event. Make it easy to remember and help your target audience see why this event is *the* right choice for them.

Finally, create your "big" promise. This bold statement summarizes your value proposition and sets the tone for your event. Your "big" promise should be attention-grabbing and memorable. It should communicate the specific outcomes that attendees can expect from your event.

Tying your value proposition and "big" promise into your event theme creates a cohesive and memorable experience for your attendees. By focusing on your target audience's critical pain points and challenges, you can create an exciting and transformational event that solves their problems and drives growth for your business.

See several samples below:

→ Discover the key strategies to skyrocket your business success. - Our event will provide a comprehensive roadmap to achieve exponential growth and reach new heights in your business ventures.

→ Elevate your business to new heights with innovative and effective strategies. - You will gain insights and tools to drive growth and success for your business.

→ Discover the key to unlocking the full potential of your business. - You will leave the event with a comprehensive strategy for driving growth and success.

→ Find the solution to unlocking your business potential and overcoming challenges. - You will leave with tailored solutions and expert advice to drive your business forward.

→ Unlock your business's full potential and achieve financial success. - You will learn proven strategies for maximizing profits and boosting your ROI.

→ Accelerate your success with the latest industry insights and techniques. - You will clearly understand how to differentiate your brand and stand out in your market.

→ Unlock the secrets to a thriving, long-lasting business. - You will leave empowered to bring your business to new heights.

→ Revamp your business with proven strategies and techniques. - You will depart from the event with a comprehensive and executable roadmap for expanding your business.

→ Enhance Your Brand and Expand Your Network: Join forces with industry peers and elevate your brand's recognition through meaningful connections.

→   Supercharge your business with the latest techniques and strategies. - You will leave our event with a wealth of knowledge and a clear roadmap for growth and success.

Now that you know how your value proposition and "big" promise play into the design of the vent, the next thing to consider is adding it to your marketing materials. Your value proposition is a crucial component of your marketing language. You can use it to entice potential attendees to register for your event.

By highlighting the specific benefits and outcomes attendees can expect from attending your event, you can create a compelling reason for them to sign up. When crafting your marketing message, be sure to focus on the unique value proposition of your event and what sets it apart from others in the industry. Emphasize the specific problems your event will solve for attendees and the benefits they will receive by attending.

This messaging should be consistent across all marketing materials, including your event website, email campaigns, social media posts, and promotional advertisements. By tying your value proposition into your marketing message, you can effectively communicate the value of your event to potential attendees and encourage them to take action.

Choosing the Ideal Location and Timing: A Guide to Selecting the Right Venue and Date for Your Event

The venue sets the event's tone and can affect your attendees' experience. The proper venue can create a positive and memorable experience for your attendees. In contrast, a poor choice of venue can lead to disappointment, dissatisfaction, and even negative reviews.

When selecting a venue, evaluate accessibility, capacity, amenities, and cost. Assess the atmosphere and ambiance of the venue and how it fits with your event's theme. To accomplish this, closely examine the venue's logistics, such as parking, transportation, and technology.

Here are some key considerations to aid in the selection of the ideal venue for your event:

Define your event needs: When selecting a venue, carefully assess your event's personality and requirements, including factors such as the type of event, the expected audience size, the planned activities, and the available budget.

Assess your audience's needs: Make sure that accessibility, transportation, and parking meet the location preferences of your target attendees. Also, assess the ambiance and atmosphere of the location to make sure that it aligns with your event's theme.

Budget: Begin by identifying potential venues that meet your event's requirements, such as size, location, and amenities. Once you have a shortlist of venues, you need to dig deeper to understand their availability and costs, which will determine whether the venue is a viable option for your event and budget.

Remember that you can often negotiate rental fees. Feel free to negotiate with venue owners or managers to secure a fair price. In addition, it's crucial to comprehend the venue's policies, including cancellation policies, alcohol policies, and space restrictions, before signing a contract.

By doing your due diligence in researching and negotiating a potential venue's rental fees and policies, you can secure the perfect location for your event while staying within budget and avoiding any surprises or hiccups on event day.

Site visit: When choosing a location for your event, it's crucial to assess the space's capacity, layout, and available amenities to verify it meets your needs. The capacity should be sufficient to accommodate your anticipated number of attendees without overcrowding or creating logistical challenges. Additionally, the layout should be conducive to your planned activities, with adequate space for your guests to move around comfortably and access all event areas.

You must pay attention to any potential logistical challenges from the location. These challenges can include accessibility for attendees with disabilities, traffic and parking considerations, and any restrictions on the use of the space. Planning for these potential challenges is vital to facilitate a smooth and successful event.

Accessibility: When selecting a suitable location for your event, you must provide accessibility to your target audience. Think about the proximity to public transportation options, parking availability, and the distance from major roads or highways.

Suppose your target audience includes individuals who rely on public transportation. If that is the case, choose a location easily accessible by bus, train, or subway to make it easy for attendees to arrive at the event on time and with minimal hassle, making their experience more positive.

For those attendees who may be driving to the event, it's worthwhile to take into account parking availability and proximity to major highways or roads. Be sure to provide clear and detailed instructions to help your attendees find the event easily.

Take a look at any potential barriers to accessibility, such as stairs or narrow walkways, make accommodations for attendees with disabilities or mobility issues, and provide accessible parking spaces, ramps, and elevators.

Unexpected scenarios: When planning an event, be proactive and anticipate any potential disruptions or unexpected challenges such as venue unavailability, inaccessibility due to unforeseen circumstances like road closures, inclement weather, or technical difficulties with equipment or services.

It is astute to create contingency plans to implement quickly and efficiently to handle disruptions. These plans can include having backup venues or locations to use if the original site is unavailable or having contingency plans for transportation or accommodations if attendees cannot access the event due to unforeseen circumstances.

It's recommended to inform attendees about your backup plans beforehand, so that in case of any unexpected disruptions, everyone is aware of what needs to be done to minimize any confusion and maintain the smooth running of the event.

Weather: It's crucial to plan for potential consequences of weather conditions on your attendees' travel to your destination. Weather-related challenges, such as inclement weather, severe storms, or other disruptions, can significantly disrupt travel schedules, making it difficult for attendees to reach the event on time.

It's prudent to have a contingency plan to overcome weather-related challenges. Be proactive and inform attendees about alternate travel routes or transportation options, rescheduling travel plans, or even delaying the event start time to allow attendees to arrive safely.

Reliable Connectivity: A solid and reliable Wi-Fi signal is crucial in today's digital age. Therefore, verify that the event space has adequate Wi-Fi to allow your attendees easy access to the internet, check emails, and stay active on social media throughout the event. Note this may require an additional cost.

In addition to Wi-Fi, verify that your team has a reliable communication source throughout the event, including using walkie-talkies or other communication devices to stay connected and quickly address any issues.

Regarding technology and staging requirements, you must determine the type of technology you and your presenters will need during the event. Assess whether the event space has the required equipment available on-site or if you need to source them from an external provider.

To make the equipment rental process smooth and hassle-free, ask your event venue to provide a list of preferred third-party providers. This will save you time in choosing the appropriate equipment for your event. It's advisable to seek recommendations from the provider on the type of equipment that suits your event and verify that they have a dependable support system in place to address any technical issues.

Verify all technical equipment, such as audio-visual equipment, microphones, projectors, screens, and lighting, is functioning correctly and is compatible with the event space. Testing the equipment before the event will prevent technical difficulties during the event.

Radio Connectivity: Don't forget to test the two-way radios before the event begins to be confident they will be effective inside the event space, especially if you're holding the event in a large venue.

Please only assume they will work after verifying beforehand so you can avoid communication breakdowns and other issues during the event. Plan to have backup communication methods, such as cell phones, in case the radios do not work as expected.

Parking: To provide hassle free parking:

1. Assess the parking options available at the venue, including the availability of covered or valet parking and any associated costs.

2. Communicate the parking details to your attendees in advance to allow them to plan accordingly. If the venue does not have sufficient parking, search for alternative options such as purchasing nearby parking lots or providing transportation from a central location.

3. Assess the lighting in the parking lot to confirm safety for late-night dismissals.

Comfort Level of Attendees: Consider the following:

1. How the venue layout will affect the flow of your event.

2. Ensuring enough restrooms, adequate ventilation, and suitable lighting for your attendees.

3. Create designated areas for specific activities, such as networking, exhibits, or presentations, if needed.

You should think about potential noise issues, such as proximity to busy streets or construction, and plan accordingly to minimize disruptions.

Lastly, it's essential to verify that the venue complies with all safety and accessibility regulations, including adequate fire exits, wheelchair access, and emergency protocols.

Food and Beverage minimums: When selecting a venue that provides catering, you need to understand the room rental and food and beverage costs. Evaluate the cost of your room rental and determine if your food and beverage expenses can offset it. Plan the meals you intend to serve at your event and negotiate your rates accordingly. If the venue has an in-house kitchen, inquire about the possibility of using your caterer or the limitations of using their preferred providers. Be aware of any surcharges or penalties incurred by opting out of their preferred caterers.

Contractual Flexibility: When negotiating your contract with the venue:

1. Pay close attention to their COVID-19 clause.

2. Confirm that you have the flexibility to postpone or reschedule your event.

3. Carefully review their Force Majeure clause and thoroughly understand its implications to avoid surprises or difficulties.

In-House Rentals: Evaluate the quality of the equipment and supplies provided by the venue to confirm that they are in good condition and meet your event standards. Double-check the rental period, pickup and delivery logistics, and any additional fees or charges if you need to rent equipment from an external company. Guarantee that the event runs smoothly by clearly communicating the venue's policies on set-up, tear-down, and cleanup to your event staff and vendors, so they understand these policies and avoid additional charges.

Evaluate the Layout and Flow: When looking for a venue for your event, you must have a clear plan for the activities and traffic flow. Before beginning your search, create a rough layout and outline the space requirements for each aspect of your event to determine if a potential venue can accommodate your needs and desired flow. Remember that you may need to be flexible, adjust the layout or flow, and be aware of any limitations of the contracted space.

Obtain Proper Licensing and Insurance Requirements: Before finalizing your venue choice:

1. Confirm the permits and insurance requirements for hosting your event.

2. Acquaint yourself with local regulations and confirm that the venue requires adequate coverage for you and your vendors.

3. Don't overlook fire code regulations that may impact your seating capacity and decor plans.

The type of permits and licensing required for live events can vary depending on the event's location and purpose. Some common types of permits and licenses you might need include:

- **Event Permit:** Depending on the size and nature of the event, you may need to obtain an event permit from the local government.

- **Alcohol Permit:** If you're serving alcohol at your event, you must obtain an alcohol permit or license from the state or local government.

- **Noise Permit:** If you're hosting a loud event, such as a concert or festival, you may need a noise permit to comply with local noise ordinances.

- **Food Permit:** If you're serving food at your event, you need a food permit from the local health department.

- **Fire Permit:** If your event involves using fireworks, open flames, or other hazardous materials, you may need a fire permit from the local fire department.

- **Park Permit:** If you're hosting an event in a public park, you may need a park permit or reservation from the local government.

- **Film Permit:** If you're filming a live event or making a documentary, you may need a film permit from the local government.

It's essential to check with the local government and other relevant authorities to determine which permits and licenses are required for your event.

Ambiance and Inclusivity: When selecting a venue for your event, it's crucial to prioritize accessibility for all attendees, including those with disabilities, to confirm that the location has required accommodations, such as ramps and accessible restrooms, and that there are no barriers to entry. Visualize the venue's atmosphere and how it aligns with your event's theme and inclusivity goals. Be mindful of any potential weather-related challenges, such as slippery surfaces, and have contingency plans to guarantee a safe and enjoyable experience.

Audio Quality: The acoustics of a venue play a critical role in the experience of your event. Ascertain the height and material of the ceilings and walls, as they can affect sound quality and create echoes or reverberation. Verify the venue has proper soundproofing and sound reinforcement systems to provide clear and consistent audio for your attendees.

Time Management:

1. Familiarize yourself with the load-in and load-out time for your event.

2. Schedule your event's and tear-down time and factor in any other events scheduled before or after yours.

3. Plan and allow adequate time for all aspects of your event, including and cleanup, to avoid unnecessary stress or delays.

Restroom accessibility and capacity: When selecting a location for your event, consider the availability and accessibility of restroom facilities for your guests. The restrooms should be adequate to accommodate the expected number of attendees. Their location should be easily accessible throughout the event space to reduce the likelihood of long lines and discomfort for your guests, which can diminish their event experience.

Additionally, for outdoor events, consider renting air-conditioned restroom trailers with running water to meet the restroom needs of your attendees.

Security Planning: Determine the security needs of your event, including the safety of your attendees, equipment, and materials. Find out if the venue provides security personnel or if you need to hire external security. Take the necessary steps to secure the event space, such as implementing crowd control and theft prevention measures. Assess the security requirements of your event and make necessary arrangements to confirm the safety of all attendees and belongings during the event.

Accommodation Arrangements: If your event is at a hotel or a similar venue, arrange for your attendees to stay nearby to me it easier for them to attend your event and participate in any activities that you have planned. You should have a backup plan. If your host hotel is at capacity, you will need to contract with another hotel or venue within easy reach of your primary event location.

Selecting the appropriate venue is crucial for a successful event, ensuring smooth execution, a positive experience for attendees, potentially enhancing attendance and engagement, and leaving a lasting impression.

However, selecting the wrong venue for your event can have a considerable effect on the success of your event. A venue that could be better suited to your event needs can lead to several issues that can negatively affect the experience for your attendees.

Let me share a story to illustrate my point. Several years ago, I worked with a client who was known for her ability to create memorable experiences. A women's group invited her to host an educational event for their members. She was excited to bring together successful and inspiring women from different industries.

She quickly secured a venue without looking at all the crucial factors. The venue was in a sketchy area on the event day with limited parking and poor accessibility. The venue was much smaller than expected, causing the room to be overcrowded and uncomfortable for attendees.

The sound system needed improvement, which made it difficult for attendees to hear the presentations. The poor lighting made it difficult to see, and it became impossible for her to repurpose any of the content from the event.

The bathroom facilities could not accommodate the high demand for breaks. Even though they converted the men's restrooms on the day of the event, her attendees were not thrilled with the men's accommodations' appearance, which led to long lines and late returns from breaks.

The portion sizes of the meals were less than expected. The catering did not meet my client's high standards, which disappointed her. Small portions and slow service added to the long list of things she wished she'd confirmed before the event.

Despite my client's best efforts to put on a good show, the event was a disaster, and many attendees left early. The attendees questioned her credibility as an event host, and, as a result, she received negative feedback from attendees.

My client learned a valuable lesson about the importance of choosing the right venue and took extra care to research all factors for her future events. She also made it a priority to get feedback from attendees to improve the experience. She wanted to avoid repeating the mistake of choosing the wrong venue.

Let's talk about how to choose a suitable time for your event. When selecting a date for your event, it's essential to check on the following:

Availability of the venue: Before finalizing the date for your event, it is crucial to double-check the available dates of your preferred venue to prevent any potential conflicts or last-minute changes that could disrupt your event planning. Check the venue's availability well in advance and be open to alternative dates if applicable.

When deciding on the date for your event, look at the schedules and availability of your target audience because it can impact attendance and the event's success, like:

- Religious holidays,
- Weekends,
- School schedules, and
- Word schedules

Select a date convenient for most of your target audience, as this will encourage higher attendance and a more engaged audience.

In addition, account for the lead time required to invite your intended audience, as it can considerably contribute to the event's turnout.

Before choosing the date for your event, research other events happening in your area. Competition from other events like trade shows, conferences, festivals, or live performances can reduce attendance, as attendees may have conflicting commitments or may choose to attend a different event instead.

Investigate the necessary lead time for securing vendors, attendees, sponsors, etc. to guarantee a successful event. Sufficient lead time enhances the chances of a smooth execution and prepares you to handle any unexpected issues.

Lastly, take into consideration the financial effects of your event date, including any potential increases in venue and vendor costs during peak seasons, and incorporate these factors into your budget. It is crucial to thoroughly understand your budget limitations and select a date that aligns with your financial parameters.

Dynamic Workshops: Harnessing the Power of Interactive Elements, Panel Discussions, and Networking

Creating engaging content that aligns with the event's goals and objectives matters when hosting a live event. The content should be well-researched and thoughtfully planned to assure attendees leave the event with valuable information and a positive experience.

There are several types of content that can be shared at a live event, let's take a closer look at each type:

Keynote speeches

A keynote is a speech or presentation that sets the tone for a live event and is typically delivered by a prominent or influential speaker. Its purpose is to inspire, motivate, or educate the audience.

The keynote is usually delivered at the beginning of the event to provide a framework for the rest of the presentations or activities. The keynote speaker usually has a unique perspective or valuable insights to share with the audience and is selected to establish the theme or objective of the event. A well-delivered keynote can leave a lasting impression on the audience and produce a positive and memorable experience for everyone involved.

Suppose you're hosting a highly attended multi-day event. Multiple keynote speakers can create a more dynamic and diverse program and keep your audience engaged and interested throughout the event. Develop an agenda in which the keynote speakers' messages align with the theme and objectives of the event while, at the same time, complementing each other.

Panel discussions

A panel discussion is a presentation where a group of experts or 'panelists' come together to discuss a specific topic or issue in front of an audience. A panel discussion aims to provide insights, perspectives, and opinions from different angles and engage the audience through interactive discussions.

During a panel discussion, the panelists are typically seated on a stage and take turns speaking, answering questions from a moderator or the audience, and conversing with each other. The moderator is responsible for guiding the discussion, keeping the panelists on track, and ensuring a balanced representation of perspectives.

A panel discussion at a live event aspires to educate, inform, and engage the audience. It provides a platform for a lively exchange of ideas, knowledge, and expertise. It creates an opportunity for the audience to ask questions, clarify their understanding, and gain a deeper appreciation of the topic. Panel discussions can generate new ideas, spark creativity, and create potential for collaboration and networking.

Workshops \ Break-out sessions

Workshops are interactive break-out sessions at live events that allow attendees to actively participate in learning through immersive hands-on activities related to a specific topic or skill. The purpose of workshops at live events is to provide attendees with the opportunity to gain practical knowledge and skills in a particular area, explore new ideas and concepts, and network and collaborate with others.

During a workshop, attendees ordinarily work in small groups, however they can work individually depending on the design of the workshop. The workshop leader guides them activities, exercises, and discussion points. Workshops can take various forms, including hands-on demonstrations, interactive lectures, problem-solving sessions, and group discussions.

Roundtable discussions

A roundtable discussion is an event where a group of people sits together at a table to discuss a specific topic or issue. A roundtable discussion facilitates open and informal discussions among participants and encourages exchanging ideas and perspectives.

In a roundtable discussion, participants sit around a table and take turns speaking, sharing their views and experiences, and conversing. Unlike a panel discussion, where there is usually a moderator and panelists, a roundtable discussion is more egalitarian, and all participants are encouraged to participate and contribute to the discussion.

A roundtable discussion at a live event aims to create a space for intimate and informal discussions among attendees. It allows attendees to network, share their experiences, and learn from each other in a relaxed and conversational setting. Roundtable discussions are beneficial for exploring complex or sensitive issues where a more formal or structured discussion may not be appropriate.

Q&A (Questions and Answers) sessions

Q&A sessions are a common feature of live events, where attendees can ask the speaker or panelists questions and receive answers. The purpose of a Q&A session is to allow attendees to clarify their understanding of the topic or issue discussed, gain additional insights and perspectives, and have their questions answered.

During a Q&A session, the speaker or panelists are typically on stage and invite the audience to ask questions using a microphone on a stand. The questions can be related to the discussed topic or more general in nature. The speaker or panelists then respond to the questions and engage in a discussion with the audience.

Awards

Awards can be given at live events to recognize and celebrate the achievements and contributions of individuals, organizations, or businesses in a specific field or industry. Giving an award or recognition at a live event is to acknowledge and honor the recipients' achievements, motivate others to strive for excellence, and create a sense of community and shared values.

Many different types of awards can be presented at live events, including:

→ **Industry awards:** These awards recognize the achievements of individuals, organizations, or businesses in a specific industry or field, such as technology, media, or arts.

→ **Performance awards:** These awards recognize outstanding performance in a specific area, such as sales, customer service, or innovation.

→ **Achievement awards:** These awards recognize noteworthy accomplishments or milestones, such as the completion of a major project, the launch of a new product, or the achievement of a personal or professional goal.

→ **Lifetime achievement awards:** These awards recognize individuals who have made a lasting contribution in their field or industry.

Awards establish and reinforce industry standards and promote the recognition of excellence and achievement. By providing a platform for recognition and celebration, awards can enhance the event experience and provide valuable insights and perspectives for attendees.

Networking

Networking time at live events allows attendees to connect and engage with each other in a relaxed and informal setting. The purpose of networking time is to facilitate the exchange of ideas, information, and experiences among attendees and to create opportunities for relationship building.

Networking time can take many forms, including coffee breaks, cocktail receptions, and organized networking activities. During these times, attendees can interact with each other, exchange business cards, and engage in conversation about their experiences, interests, and perspectives. Networking helps attendees develop a sense of community and build a network of contacts they can call upon for support and collaboration in the future.

VIP (Very Important Person) Experiences

VIP experiences are exclusive and premium options offered at live events for select attendees. VIP experiences provide attendees with a more personalized and elevated experience at the event and offer a range of exclusive benefits and privileges.

VIP experiences can include a range of benefits and privileges, such as:

→ **Early access to the event:** Offering early access to VIPs is a common practice in event planning because it is an attractive perk for those who are willing to pay a premium price for VIP treatment. By allowing VIPs to enter the event before the general public, they can have a chance to explore the event space and participate in activities before the crowds arrive and can provide VIPs with an opportunity to interact with event organizers and keynote speakers in a more intimate setting. Offering early access to VIPs can enhance the exclusivity and perceived value of the event.

→ **Exclusive seating**: VIPs may have the privilege to access exclusive seating areas with better views of the stage or other important areas of the event. These areas may offer additional comfort or amenities like comfortable seating, private restrooms, and dedicated food and beverage services.

→ **Private hospitality**: VIPs may access exclusive meet-and-greet sessions with event speakers, performers, or industry leaders, allowing one-on-one interactions and potential collaborations.

Additionally, VIPs may receive complimentary gifts or merchandise, such as event swag bags or branded merchandise, as a token of appreciation for their attendance and support. This level of exclusivity and personalized attention can create a sense of loyalty and excitement among VIP attendees, further enhancing the success and reputation of the event.

→ **Special events and activities**: VIPs may access exclusive perks like unique gift bags, personalized experiences, or concierge services. These perks can make VIPs feel valued and appreciated. They may encourage them to attend future events or recommend your event to others. Additionally, VIPs may be able to participate in exclusive workshops or educational sessions led by industry experts, providing them with valuable insights and knowledge. Offering VIP experiences enhances the quality of your event and creates a memorable experience for attendees.

→ **Premium amenities**: VIPs may receive access to exceptional amenities not available to the general public, such as VIP-only parking or valet services. They might receive personalized attention from event staff, such as dedicated VIP customer service or concierge support. Additionally, VIPs may be granted exclusive discounts for future events or related products/services.

The purpose of VIP experiences in live events is to provide attendees with a more personalized and elevated experience at the event. By offering exclusive benefits and privileges, VIP experiences can enhance the event experience and provide attendees with a unique and memorable experience they will cherish for a long time.

Regardless of the type of the content shared, prioritize the audience's needs and confirm that the content is both accessible and engaging. The use of visual aids, such as slideshows, videos, or candid moments caught on camera, can engage attendees and make the content more memorable.

It is crucial to take into account the length of the event, the content shared, the time of day, and the audience's energy levels to make sure that the event runs smoothly and attendees leave with a positive experience.

What type of event should you host?

The best types of events to grow your business depend on your business's specific goals and needs. Before you start planning an event, it is crucial to be clear about your "why" and clearly outline your goals. Taking time to pause and get clear will make it easy to choose which event type is right for you.

Check out the different types of events and business objectives they can help you achieve:

1. **Networking Events:**

   Networking events bring together individuals from different businesses and industries to establish new relationships, exchange information and ideas, and promote their businesses and products.

   Networking events create opportunities for attendees to connect with others in their industry, build relationships, and promote their brands and products. If your business is centered around fostering connections, hosting networking events can be a highly effective tool to drive growth and success.

   Many types of businesses can benefit from attending networking events, including:

   a. **Small businesses:** Networking events allow small businesses to connect with potential customers, partners, and suppliers.

   b. **Start-ups**: Networking events can help start-ups build relationships with potential investors, partners, and customers.

   c. **Professional services firms:** Networking events can provide professional services firms, such as law firms and consulting firms, with an opportunity to connect with potential clients and referral sources.

   d. **Sales and marketing professionals:** Networking events allow sales and marketing professionals to connect with potential customers and partners.

   e. **Nonprofits:** Networking events allow nonprofits to connect with potential donors, volunteers, and partners.

   f. **Entrepreneurs:** Networking events can allow entrepreneurs to connect with potential investors, customers, and partners.

2. **Workshops and Seminars**:

A workshop or seminar aims to provide attendees with educational and informative content on a specific topic or issue. Workshops and seminars provide attendees hands-on learning experiences and help them gain new skills, knowledge, and perspectives.

By hosting workshops and seminars, business owners can establish themselves as thought leaders in their industry, build relationships with their target audience, and promote their products and services.

Many types of businesses can benefit from hosting workshops or seminars, including:

a. **Training and development organizations:** Workshops and seminars can provide training and development organizations with an opportunity to offer their services to a broader audience.

b. **Professional services firms:** Workshops and seminars can provide professional services firms, such as consulting firms and law firms, with an opportunity to showcase their expertise and connect with potential clients.

c. **Education and training providers**: Workshops and seminars can provide education and training providers with an opportunity to promote their programs and connect with potential students.

d. **Nonprofits**: Workshops and seminars allow nonprofits to educate their stakeholders and promote their cause.

e. **Industry associations:** Workshops and seminars allow industry associations to educate their members and promote their industry.

f. **Corporations:** Workshops and seminars allow corporations to educate employees and promote their brands.

3. **Product Launches:**

A product launch aims to introduce a new product or service to the market and generate excitement and interest around the product.

A product launch is a marketing event designed to showcase the features and benefits of the product, demonstrate its use, and encourage attendees to purchase the product. By hosting a product launch, businesses can generate excitement and interest around their new product, build relationships with their target audience, and increase sales.

Many types of businesses can benefit from hosting a product launch, including:

a. **Coaches and Consultants:** Coaches and consultants can showcase their expertise, build relationships with their target audience, generate leads, establish thought leadership, and offer training and education on their products and services. Whether you are a coach, consultant, or service provider, a product launch event can provide valuable opportunities for growth and success.

As a caveat, many coaches and consultants use product launches to launch their new book. This type of event can generate sales and create momentum that can lead to book signing events.

b. **Professional services companies:** Professional services companies can showcase their expertise, build relationships with their target audience, generate leads, establish thought leadership, and offer training and education on their products and services. Whether you are a financial services firm, law firm, or accounting firm, a product launch event can provide valuable opportunities for growth and success.

c. **Technology, Pharmaceutical, Automotive, Consumer Goods, and Retail companies:** Tech companies can showcase their innovation, generate excitement and interest around their products, generate leads, establish thought leadership, and offer hands-on demonstrations. Whether you are a software company, hardware company, or consumer electronics company, a product launch can provide valuable opportunities for growth and success.

4. **Customer Appreciation Events:**

   A customer appreciation event's purpose is to show customers gratitude for their loyalty and support.

   Customer appreciation events provide opportunities for companies to connect with their customers, build relationships, and show appreciation for their business. Be sure to include exclusive discounts, access to new products or services, or special perks.

5. **Charity and Community Events:**

   Hosting a charity or community event is to raise awareness and funds for a specific cause or charity.

   Charity events provide a platform for businesses to give back to their communities, demonstrate their commitment to social responsibility, and engage with their customers and employees in a meaningful way. Whether you are a retail company, service company, technology company, consumer goods company, or pharmaceutical company, a charity or community event can provide valuable opportunities for growth and success.

6. **Retreats:**

   The purpose of a retreat is to provide a change of scenery and a focused, distraction-free environment for employees, business partners , or clients to come together, collaborate, and re-energize.

Retreats provide a space for businesses to reflect on their goals and strategies, foster teamwork and collaboration, and improve employee morale and satisfaction. Retreats offer a unique opportunity to connect with your customers on a more personal level. You can use the retreat to get to know your customers, listen to their feedback, and build stronger relationships.

Retreats are particularly well suited for coaches and consultants to create profoundly transformative client experiences. However, many industries could benefit from hosting this style of event.

Keep in mind, the best type of event for your business will depend on your specific goals, target audience, and resources. Always plan and execute your events carefully and thoughtfully to ensure they succeed and achieve your desired outcomes.

Creating an Engaging and Memorable Event Experience

A memorable event can help you achieve your business goals by creating a positive and lasting impression on attendees and by fostering engagement and relationships with your target audience.

Memorable can be subjective, so let me share some examples of memorable events I've designed over the years:

Big-name entertainment: Having a surprise reveal at your events is always fun. At one of my events, we surprised the attendees with the B-52s. Seeing their faces when the event host introduced the band to their high-end project reveal event was delightful.

This client made it part of the culture for their annual event to have surprise elements so their attendees would expect each year to be better than the previous year.

Unusual experiences: Two of my clients were brothers who owned rival insurance agencies. They hosted an annual employee appreciation event for their sales teams and families. One year, they wanted to really WOW their attendees, so they planned a professional ice skating show with dinner served literally on the ice. Elegantly dressed tables were placed around the ice rink's perimeter, and the skaters performed in the middle of the tables. The attendees were in awe of the skaters' skills and thrilled to participate in such a unique event.

Once-in-a-lifetime opportunities: I had the incredible opportunity to live in a city that hosted the Olympic Training Center and that trained athletes in several popular sports. I was able to recreate Olympic competitions featuring athlete demonstrations and the attendees as the competitors. It was one of the BIGGEST WOW factors I had the privilege of planning and facilitating.

Community Service: Many corporate clients wanted to give back to the community, so we'd host annual build-a-bike events that served as team building for the corporation's employees. Each team would be responsible for building 2 - 3 bikes in a set time frame. At the end of the event, they would present bikes to an organization that catered to disadvantaged youth. It was a tremendous way to break up the monotony of several meeting days, bring great press to their organization. Win/Win/Win

Red Carpet: One of my smaller clients wanted her attendees to feel like Hollywood stars. The opening event featured photographers taking glam shots as they entered the event space. A branded wall (step and repeat) provided an exciting backdrop for photo ops. The attendees were excited to share their experiences on social media. Her brand blew up! Her attendees loved the way she made them feel, and it built an incredible desire for future attendees to sign up.

Here are some ways in which a memorable event can enable you to achieve your business goals:

Building brand awareness: Creating unforgettable client experiences can elevate your brand and expand your reach. By providing unique and engaging experiences, your clients will be more likely to share their positive experiences with others to increase brand awareness and build a sense of community.

Evaluate how you can showcase your products and services in a way that leaves a lasting impression on your clients and incorporates interactive elements, personalized touches, or exclusive perks for attendees. When all is said and done, creating memorable experiences can differentiate your brand and establish it as a leader in your industry.

Generating leads: By designing an event that genuinely resonates with your audience, you can create a unique experience that leaves a lasting impact and includes elements, such as workshops, games, or hands-on activities, and leveraging technology to enhance the event experience. By doing so, you can differentiate yourself from competitors and attract a wider audience while strengthening your brand reputation and cultivating customer loyalty.

Fostering relationships: Creating a sense of community at your event can be accomplished through icebreakers, group discussions, and networking sessions.

By encouraging attendees to interact and engage with one another, you can facilitate the formation of relationships that extend beyond the event itself and be beneficial for your attendees and your business, as it can lead to new partnerships, collaborations, and opportunities for growth.

By building a solid community around your brand, you can establish yourself as a trusted and respected leader in your industry, leading to increased brand recognition and customer loyalty.

Educating attendees: Provide attendees with a rich and valuable learning experience by offering interactive workshops, training sessions, and keynote presentations.

These opportunities can equip attendees with the tools and knowledge to succeed in their respective fields while establishing your brand as a valuable resource and an expert in the industry.

Encourage attendees to participate in Q&A sessions, panel discussions, or roundtable conversations, enabling them to engage with thought leaders in their fields and ask questions in real time. You can provide attendees access to post-event resources, such as webinars to continue their learning and keep your brand top-of-mind.

By providing valuable educational experiences, you can cultivate a sense of trust and loyalty with your attendees and establish your event as a must-attend for professionals in your industry.

Enhancing customer loyalty: Strengthen customer relationships and improve loyalty by delivering a memorable event experience. Creating positive and engaging experiences for attendees will foster new relationships and reinforce existing ones, leading to increased loyalty and repeat business for your brand.

Maximize the effect of your event by creating a memorable experience. Whether your goal is to educate attendees, promote your brand, or build relationships, an extraordinary event can help you achieve your objectives and leave a lasting impression on your audience.

Several elements contribute to a memorable event, including:

Engaging content: Your content should be relevant, thought-provoking, and tailored to the interests and needs of the audience.

You can achieve this by including a mix of dynamic keynote speeches, insightful panel discussions, and interactive break-out sessions. These sessions should encourage active participation and facilitate learning and growth.

By offering high-quality content, you will enhance your attendees' experience and create a memorable event that leaves a lasting impact

Interactive experiences: By incorporating engagement opportunities, attendees are more likely to be invested in the event and leave with a sense of accomplishment and value.

Additionally, this can develop a sense of community and increase the likelihood of attendees returning for future events. Use event apps or social media to enhance engagement, facilitate real-time feedback and communication, and provide valuable data and insights to improve future events.

Unique and memorable experiences: Elevate your event to the next level by providing attendees with unique and unforgettable experiences they will cherish long after the event. From exclusive meet-and-greets with industry leaders to behind-the-scenes tours of your venue, these special touches will leave a lasting impression on attendees and set your event apart from the rest. By creating these one-of-a-kind experiences, you'll engage and captivate your audience and establish your brand as a leader in your industry.

High-quality production: Take your event to the next level by investing in professional event production and high-quality audio-visual components. Deliver an immersive experience that engages and captivates attendees with clear sound systems, stunning visuals, and expertly coordinated lighting and technical elements. Demonstrating your commitment to excellence and attention to detail will elevate your brand and create a truly unforgettable event.

Personalized touch: By taking the time to gather feedback and understand the preferences and interests of your attendees, you can customize the event experience to meet your attendees' individual needs.

For example, suppose your attendees are primarily tech-savvy millennials. In that case, you should incorporate interactive technology and social media into the event design.

Alternatively, suppose your attendees are primarily professionals in a specific industry. In that case, you should focus on offering educational and networking opportunities specific to their field.

Incorporating these personalized elements into the event can create a more engaging and memorable experience for each attendee.

Networking opportunities: Encourage attendees to connect and build relationships by providing opportunities for networking and collaboration. These opportunities will enhance the attendee experience and create meaningful connections and relationships that attendees can leverage beyond the event.

Memorable branding: Make a lasting impression and reinforce your brand by incorporating it into the event in a memorable and transformational way. Prominent event signage, eye-catching promotional materials, and valuable branded merchandise can help you accomplish this objective. These elements will reinforce your brand and increase visibility, leave a lasting impression on attendees, and serve as a tangible reminder of the event experience.

To achieve a cohesive event design, analyze your event's theme and purpose, and confirm that all elements, including the venue and decorations, are aligned with the theme. Strive to create an atmosphere that is welcoming and inclusive, and prioritize the comfort and enjoyment of your attendees.

Incorporate elements of surprise and delight to enhance the attendee experience, such as unexpected entertainment or unique interactive activities that create a buzz and generate enthusiasm for your event, leading to positive word-of-mouth marketing and increased attendance.

Finally, leverage technology to enhance the attendee experience through event apps or live streaming, and utilize social media to promote your event and engage with attendees before, during, and after the event. A well-executed and memorable event can increase revenue, brand awareness, and customer loyalty, making it a worthwhile investment for any business.

Event Planning Tools: Essential Tools for a Successful Event

*P*lanning and executing an event can be overwhelming if you don't have organization and structure in place. Each task needs to be accounted for and assigned to a responsible party. No one can plan an event on their own, so before you get started, take an inventory of the skills you need on your team to design a profitable event.

Planning tools can help produce a successful event, including:

Budget: An event budget is a comprehensive financial tool that outlines all of the costs associated with the event, including venue rental, catering, audio-visual equipment, and any other expenses. A budget keeps you on track financially and all costs are accounted for.

Creating and keeping a budget updated will aid in financial planning, cost control, forecasting, and decision-making, allowing for better negotiating. You need to know your numbers to run a successful and profitable event.

As you build out your budget, you'll want to track costs for:

- Venue

- Food and Beverage

- AV

- Decor

- Marketing and promotions

- Staff

- Transportation

- Lodging

- Gifts

- Rentals: tables, chairs, linens, etc

Event timeline and task list: An event timeline is a comprehensive schedule that outlines all tasks and deadlines that must be completed before, during, and after the event. This tool keeps everyone in the event planning process organized and on track.

I like using Trello, Asana, or ClickUp to organize the project timeline and tasks. These apps make planning easy. You can track deadlines, links to documents and photos, and keep all communication in one place to streamline processes.

A spreadsheet works fine for smaller events. However, it can get large, complicated to manage, and out of control as the project progresses if you host large events with complex moving parts. And, as much as I love spreadsheets, it is more practical to use an app that can handle massive amounts of updates efficiently.

Venue diagram: A venue diagram is a visual representation of the event space, including the placement of tables, chairs, and other elements. This tool confirms that the event space is functional, aesthetically pleasing, and aligns with the event's goals and objectives.

Contact list: A contact list is a comprehensive list of all of the contacts that are involved in the event, including vendors, attendees, and stakeholders. This tool guarantees that all relevant parties are informed and kept up-to-date throughout the event planning process. This list can be included as part of the Run of Show to keep things organized and have easy access.

Run of Show: Developing a Run of Show (ROS) is a vital aspect of event planning that requires careful attention and detailed organization. It is a good idea to start developing a ROS as soon as possible in the planning process, ideally several months before the event.

The precise timeline for creating a ROS (Run of Show) may differ based on the event's scale and intricacy, but it's typically recommended to start early to guarantee that all event elements are thoroughly considered and accounted for in the schedule.

I typically have two versions of the ROS. One is used for the AV and backstage team to keep the event on time and run smoothly. The second version is one I use on-site with my meeting planner to track all of the happenings from the time we hit the ground until we leave.

Here are some general guidelines to follow:

- **Start with a draft:**

  Start with a rough draft of the Run of Show as soon as possible in the planning process, even if it is incomplete. It will identify potential issues or conflicts early on and adjust as needed.

- **Revise as needed:**

  As you continue to plan and make decisions about the event, revise the Run of Show as needed to accurately reflect the event schedule and details.

- **Finalize the Run of Show:**

  Set a goal to finalize the Run of Show several weeks before the event to allow time for any adjustments or revisions.

The Run of Show should be a living and breathing document that is started early in the planning process and updated with all event changes. It holds the answers to all of the questions about the event flow. Key players on the event team need to have a fresh copy daily.

Let's take a closer look at some of the most popular event-planning apps:

Trello is my favorite project management tool. It is easy to use for event planning. Most of the teams I work with can use it easily. It keeps track of tasks and deadlines as well as facilitates team collaboration.

Here's a quick step-by-step process of how to use Trello for event planning:

1. **Create a Board:** Create a new board in Trello and give it a name that reflects your event, such as "Event X Planning."

2. **Set up Lists:** Within the board, create lists that reflect the different stages of the event planning process. For example, you could have lists for "Ideas," "To Do," "In Progress," and "Completed."

3. **Add Cards:** Under each list, add cards that represent individual tasks. For example, under the "To Do" list, you could add a card for "Book Venue."

4. **Assign Members:** Assign team members to each card so everyone knows what tasks they are responsible for.

5. **Add Details:** Add details to each card, such as a due date, description, and attachments. You can also use checklists and labels to categorize further and organize tasks.

6. **Monitor Progress**: Use Trello's drag-and-drop feature to move cards from one list to another as tasks are completed. This system tracks the progress of the event planning process and ensures everything is accounted for..

7. **Collaborate**: Trello allows for real-time collaboration so that team members can communicate and share information directly within the tool.

Trello makes it easy to share information at a glance. Each card makes it easy to categorize tasks and move list items around.

Asana is another easy-to-use app for event management. It can be set up in a kanban style and function like Trello. And it has a collaboration feature that is an excellent addition:

The following steps can help you use Asana to plan and manage your event:

1. **Create a Project:** Start by creating a new project in Asana and name it after your event.

2. **Add Team Members:** IInvite team members and any relevant stakeholders to the project to collaborate and communicate with each other.

3. **Define Tasks**: Create a list of tasks that need to be completed for the event, such as venue booking, catering, and vendor management. Assign each task to a team member and set deadlines.

4. **Track Progress:** Use Asana's task list and calendar view to track the progress of each task and confirm that everything is on track.

5. **Communicate:** Use Asana's built-in commenting and messaging system to communicate with team members and stakeholders. You can attach files and images to your tasks to keep all relevant information in one place.

6. **Stay Organized:** Use tags and custom fields to organize tasks and track important information, such as budget and vendor contacts.

7. **Monitor Deadlines:** Use Asana's calendar view to monitor deadlines and track tasks through completion.

8. **Collaborate:** Asana's collaboration features allow you to work with your team to plan and execute a successful event. You can use Asana's mobile app to stay connected and on top of your event planning tasks while on the go.

ClickUp is probably the most powerful of the apps I've mentioned here. I especially appreciate how it keeps all communication in an easy-to-read thread for each task item.

ClickUp is a project management and productivity tool that makes event planning easy. The platform provides a centralized place for event planners to organize tasks, communicate with team members, and track progress. Here's how you can set up ClickUp for event planning:

1. **Create a new project:** Start by creating a new project in Click-Up specifically for your event.

2. **Assign tasks:** Create tasks for each aspect of the event, such as venue selection, catering, entertainment, etc. Assign tasks to team members or delegate them to sub-tasks.

3. **Collaborate:** Collaborate with your team members in re-al-time using the platform's comments and messaging features. You have the ability to mention team members in tasks to keep them updated.

4. **Set deadlines:** Set deadlines for each task, keep everyone on track so that the event runs smoothly.

5. **Manage your budget:** Use ClickUp's custom fields to track your budget and expenses and monitor your event's financial status.

6. **Track progress**: Use ClickUp's status updates and progress reports to track each task's progress and the event.

7. **Document mission-critical information:** Store event information, such as vendor contracts, floor plans, and guest lists, in ClickUp's file section.

Using ClickUp for event planning, you can streamline the planning process and reduce the risk of mistakes.

There are dozens of options available, including Trello, Asana, and ClickUp. These tools all work similarly, providing a platform to keep track of tasks, deadlines, and team members' progress. The main objective is to choose a tool you and your team will use.

Assembling Your Dream Team: Building a Strong Event Planning Squad

*Y*ou will need a team with diverse skills to plan and execute your live events. Some of those skills include event planning and coordination, marketing and promotion, graphic design and copywriting, logistics and operations, and project management.

An event planner plays a crucial role in planning and executing a successful event. They work behind the scenes to plan and coordinate all the details that make your vision come to life.

To plan and execute your own events, you will need a team with a range of skills, including:

Event planner: As mentioned, an event planner can manage event logistics and ensure everything runs smoothly. They are not "the" visionary in the planning process, but they execute the plans that turn your vision into a reality.

Project manager: A project manager is a valued member of an event planning team, especially if you're planning large-scale events. Their main responsibility is to ensure that all event elements come together seamlessly. While an event planner focuses on the creative and logistical aspects of the event, a project manager's role is to oversee the planning and execution of the entire event from start to finish.

The project manager is responsible for developing a project plan, creating timelines, and ensuring all tasks are completed on time and within budget. They work closely with the event planner to ensure that the event meets all the goals and objectives of the client.

Additionally, a project manager is responsible for identifying potential risks and developing contingency plans to minimize any adverse effects on the event. Collaborating with vendors and contractors guarantees that all deliverables are fulfilled and maintain the required quality standards.

Marketing and communications: Having a marketing and communication specialist on your event planning team is crucial for ensuring the success of your event. This professional is responsible for creating and implementing a marketing and communication strategy to promote the event and attract attendees.

A marketing and communication team member will work closely with the event planner to identify the target audience, create a messaging strategy, and develop promotional materials such as flyers, social media posts, and email campaigns. They should manage communication with attendees before, during, and after the event, including providing information about the schedule, speakers, and logistics.

This role should focus on building brand awareness and engagement with attendees by developing engaging and interactive content for social media and other digital platforms.

They can analyze the event's performance metrics and feedback to make adjustments and improvements for future events.

Copywriter: While a marketing and communication specialist is responsible for developing and executing marketing strategies to promote an event or business, a copywriter is responsible for creating the written content that goes into those marketing materials.

Copywriters specialize in crafting compelling and persuasive language that engages and persuades the target audience. They work closely with marketing and communication specialists to ensure that the copy (sales page, emails, other promotional materials) aligns with the marketing strategy and effectively communicates the intended message.

To clarify, a marketing and communication specialist is responsible for the strategy. At the same time, a copywriter focuses on the language used to convey that strategy to the target audience.

Copywriters can be expensive, but a great copywriter is worth their weight in gold when it comes to recouping your ROI. I recommend you have a skilled copywriter on your team.

Graphic designer: An excellent graphic designer is essential for creating a solid brand identity for your event and business. They can create visually appealing logos, marketing materials, and event signage that effectively communicates your brand message and values to your target audience.

A well-designed brand will help you stand out, build credibility, and increase brand recognition. Your designer can create consistent and cohesive visuals across your marketing materials, creating a professional and polished image for your event or business.

Caterer: If you are serving food at your event, a caterer can assist you with menu planning, source ingredients, and provide staffing for the event.

Audio-visual specialist: An audio-visual specialist can guide you through all the technical aspects of your event, including sound, lighting, and video.

A good AV (audio-visual) specialist can significantly enhance the quality of your event by providing professional sound, lighting, and video production services.

They are instrumental in finding creative solutions to technical challenges to achieve your audience's desired atmosphere.

Suppose you're looking to repurpose your content. In that case, hiring the venue's AV team may not be adequate, so fully assess your needs before making a hiring decision. It may be in your best interest to pay more to get the ROI you're looking for in this area.

Event Decorator/designer: A decor house or event production company can design and create the visual elements of your event, including flowers, centerpieces, and other decorations.

Decor sets the tone and atmosphere for the occasion. It creates a visual and sensory experience for attendees, making them feel welcomed and engaged. A well-designed event can enhance the theme and create a cohesive look and feel.

Decor can highlight different aspects of the event, such as sponsors or keynote speakers. It can even serve as a branding opportunity for your organization.

A well-designed stage is crucial to the aesthetics of a live event. It is the focal point and sets the tone for the entire event. A visually appealing stage can create a positive and memorable experience for attendees. In contrast, a poorly designed stage can detract from the event atmosphere and underwhelm attendees.

A well-designed stage enhances the theme or message of the event. The setting can display logos, graphics, and branding elements to reinforce the event's content, so that your attendees connect with the theme, and guarantee a cohesive and immersive experience.

A well-designed stage can improve the production quality of the event. It can provide a platform for speakers and performers and create a professional and polished atmosphere to increase the event's perceived value, making attendees more likely to return in the future.

I cannot overstate the importance of a well-designed stage. It is the focal point of every successful event. It should be carefully considered and planned for to create a positive and memorable experience for all attendees.

Volunteer coordinator: If you plan to use volunteers at your event, a volunteer coordinator can recruit, train, and manage them. Your meeting planner can handle this duty if you need more room in your budget for dedicated staff. Suppose you're running a small event with at most ten volunteers. In that case, you can contact local community leaders to secure the human resources needed to staff your event.

Legal advisor: A legal advisor can assist you with any legal issues related to your event, including contracts, liability, and insurance.

Many small business owners lack financial resources to hire an attorney to review contracts. There are several alternatives for having a second set of eyes look at your contracts to make sure all of your bases are covered:

- Use a contract review service.
- Consult with a business advisor who has experience with your type of contract. You may find a resource through SCORE. Ask your local Chamber of Commerce.
- Utilize contract review platforms like LegalZoom or Rocket Lawyer for affordable pricing.
- Hire a paralegal.
- Check out LegalShield's subscription service to see if their services cover your contract review needs.

Financial advisor: A financial advisor can assist you with budgeting, fundraising, and managing the financial aspects of your event.

Let's face it, the last thing most small business owners want to do is spend time doing their books. But it's imperative that you know your numbers throughout each phase of the planning process.

A bookkeeper or accountant is needed for running successful events because they can manage your finances, keep accurate records. They can track expenses, handle invoicing, and manage your cash flow, ensuring your event runs smoothly and profitably.

In addition, a bookkeeper or accountant can identify tax deductions to comply with all applicable tax laws and regulations. By having a bookkeeper or accountant on your team, you can focus on the creative aspects of your event while they handle the financial details.

While having a large team may seem overwhelming, you'll want to focus on much needed skill sets when assembling your event planning team.

Sometimes, one person can fulfill multiple roles, especially if you're hosting a small event. Remember, having a well-rounded team with the skills to execute a successful event is key.

Your event's scale and intricacy will determine your team's size. You may have to hire more staff or contractors to fulfill specific roles during portions of the planning cycle.

I must emphasize that having the right people with the appropriate skills and expertise on your team will reduce stress and make your life easier, even if you're hosting small events.

The Roadmap to a Successful Event: Understanding Your Timeline and Run of Show

*P*lanning a large-scale live event can be an intimidating project. Still, by breaking it down into manageable steps and starting early, you can create an event that is successful and enjoyable for all involved.

Here are some key components to keep in mind during the **6-12 months leading up to your event**:

Define your event goals and objectives: Understanding your goals will guide the planning process, ensuring that all decisions align with the desired outcome. You can determine the target audience, appropriate marketing strategies, and selected event format by clearly defining what you hope to achieve. Knowing your event goals will assist in allocating the budget, vendor selection, and logistics.

Establish your event budget and revenue goals: A detailed budget will identify your event's costs, such as venue rental, food and beverage, marketing, and staff, and track cash flow required to cover each expense. Moreover, budgeting can keep costs under control and avoid overspending, which can impact your bottom line.

By tracking your expenses against your budget, you can make informed decisions about where to allocate resources and cut back. A well-thought-out budget can keep costs under control and maximize revenue and profitability for your event.

Choose the event date and location: Selecting a date and location early in the event planning allows you to secure the best venue for your event and avoid potential conflicts with other events.

By booking a venue early, you can negotiate better rates, confirm that the space meets your needs, and enable you to plan other event elements, such as catering and decor, with more certainty while giving your guests ample time to plan and prepare the event. Securing a prime location can attract more attendees and generate higher revenue.

Research and secure vendors and suppliers: Researching and booking speakers or entertainment early in the planning cycle will give you more time to negotiate fees and finalize contracts. It also increases the likelihood that the speakers or entertainment you want to feature will be available on your event date. It may result in higher fees or settling for a less desirable option if you wait until the last minute to book speakers or entertainment.

Develop the event concept and theme: The event concept and theme play a crucial role in shaping the experience of the event, from branding and marketing to decor and activities. To make your event more dynamic and engaging, choosing a theme that resonates with your event goals and target audience is crucial to creating a cohesive and impactful experience that leaves a lasting impression on your attendees.

Furthermore, the chosen theme will influence decisions regarding the venue, vendors, and other aspects of event planning. A well-executed theme can enhance the attendee experience and leave a lasting impression. By carefully considering and incorporating the theme throughout the event, you can create a truly immersive and memorable experience for your attendees.

Research and book speakers or entertainment: Researching and booking speakers or entertainment early will give you more time to negotiate fees and finalize contracts. This will ensure that the speakers or entertainment you want to feature are available on the date of your event. Keep in mind, it can take months to get a signed contract with a celebrity speaker.

Develop your marketing plan and start promoting your event: Developing a marketing plan that includes a mix of tactics such as social media promotion, email marketing, public relations, and paid advertising can help you reach your target audience and generate excitement around your event.

Use persuasive messaging and compelling visuals to communicate the value and benefits of attending your event. Offer early bird discounts or other incentives to encourage attendees to purchase tickets.

Create an event website or landing page: Having a dedicated website or landing page for your event will make it easier for attendees to learn more about your event and provide a platform to register and purchase tickets.

The website should include all relevant event information, such as date, time, location, registration details, and engaging visuals and content that accurately reflects the event theme and concept.

Additionally, the website can serve as a hub for event updates, sponsor recognition, and post-event content.

Develop your registration process and ticketing system: Creating an efficient and user-friendly registration process and ticketing system is essential to deliver a hassle-free check-in process for attendees.

It should include providing clear instructions and guidelines for registration, offering various ticket options and payment methods, and utilizing a reliable event management software or platform to manage registrations and ticketing.

A seamless registration and ticketing process will enhance the attendee experience, save time, and reduce stress for event organizers.

Start planning your event schedule and agenda: Keeping a detailed event schedule and agenda will keep you on track during the planning process and help you complete all tasks promptly.

It will communicate much needed information to vendors, sponsors, and attendees and give them a clear understanding of what to expect from the event.

Moreover, a detailed agenda can help identify possible scheduling conflicts or gaps in the program, enabling you to make adjustments that ensure a positive and engaging experience for attendees.

Obtain permits or licenses: Obtaining proper permits or licenses will guarantee that your event complies with local regulations and laws.

Depending on the location and nature of the event, you may need to secure permits for parking, alcohol sales, sound, or use of public spaces.

Research and understand all pertinent permit and license requirements well in advance to avoid any last-minute issues.

As the event date approaches, you must finalize all details to ensure a successful event. Here are some key tasks to focus on **4-6 months before the event:**

Finalize the event schedule and agenda: Planning and effectively communicating the event details with vendors, suppliers, and attendees will put everyone on the same page, resulting in a seamless event execution.

Provide clear information on schedules, deadlines, and expectations and schedule regular check-ins and updates to keep everyone informed.

By establishing clear lines of communication and proactively addressing any potential issues, you can avoid last-minute surprises.

Finalize vendor and supplier contracts: To avoid misunderstandings or conflicts later in the planning process, execute all contracts outlining all details clearly, including payment terms, deadlines, and any other pertinent information related to the vendors or suppliers.

Create a detailed event budget and track expenses: Create a spreadsheet or budget tracker to keep track of all costs associated with the event. These should include all vendor and supplier fees, marketing and advertising costs, rental fees, and other expenses. Regularly review the budget tracker to make sure you stay within your budget and make adjustments as needed to avoid overspending. Keeping all receipts and invoices organized and easily accessible for future reference is important.

Start building relationships with event sponsors and partners: Create partnerships with businesses and organizations that can expand your event's reach and attract new attendees.

Look for organizations that align with your event's theme or mission, and work with them to create mutually beneficial promotional opportunities.

For example, you could partner with a local restaurant to offer attendees discounts or work with a nonprofit organization to raise awareness and funds for a related cause.

You can leverage their networks and resources to make your event successful by collaborating with others.

Develop and implement your social media plan: Social media can be a powerful tool to generate buzz, increase attendance, and engage with your target audience before, during, and after the event.

Develop a social media strategy that includes promoting the event on relevant platforms, sharing engaging content and updates, running social media contests, and interacting with attendees and sponsors.

A well-constructed social media plan can create a sense of community around your event and foster engagement with your brand.

Plan and book event transportation: Consider transportation options for attendees, speakers, and sponsors. Research the best modes of transportation, such as shuttle buses or taxis, and book them in advance to provide smooth and efficient transportation services for all involved.

Provide parking options or arranging valet services to make it easy for guests to get to the event location.

Develop your event security plan: Develop a comprehensive security plan that addresses potential risks and threats, such as fire hazards, medical emergencies, and potential security breaches.

Train event staff and volunteers on how to respond to these situations and put emergency procedures in place. Conduct a thorough risk assessment of the event space and take steps to mitigate potential risks.

Plan your event signage and branding: Creating consistent visual branding across all event materials, such as promotional items, signage, and marketing materials, can increase brand awareness and recognition.

By choosing a cohesive color scheme, typography, and design elements, attendees will quickly recognize and associate the event with your brand.

In the **2-4 months before the event,** the focus shifts towards finalizing key details and preparing for the event's logistics.

A critical task during this period is to finalize all speaker or entertainment contracts to ensure that all performers or presenters are fully committed to the event.

Finalize all catering arrangements, including menu selections and dietary requirements, pay close attention to allergens and food sensitivities so you can accommodate all attendees.

Coordinate the timing of the meals with the event schedule to avoid any disruptions or delays. Finally, ensuring that the food and beverage presentation will be visually appealing and in line with the event theme can elevate the attendees' experience and add to the event's success.

Developing and implementing an event volunteer plan is crucial during this period. Volunteers play a meaningful role in the success of an event, and a well-planned volunteer program can facilitate the event flow so that everything runs smoothly.

Another critical consideration is the event's setup and layout. It's time to solidify the placement of chairs, tables, and other equipment, create a floor plan, and decide on the event's flow.

Finalize audio-visual and technology requirements, including equipment or software.

In the **final month leading up to the event**, verify all details are in place and confirmed.

Event walk-through: Conduct a final event venue walk-through to verify all agreed-upon arrangements are in place. This walk-through is the last opportunity to confirm all vendor and supplier arrangements and any travel or lodging arrangements for speakers or entertainment. I recommend using this opportunity to address any last-minute changes.

Load in / load out schedule: It is essential to develop an event timeline and load-in/load-out schedules during this time. These schedules will guarantee that everything runs smoothly on the event day.

Registration/reminders:

Review the registration and ticketing process and send final reminders and updates to minimize any last-minute confusion or issues.

In the **final week leading up to your event** conduct a thorough review of all event logistics to ensure everything is in place for the event.

Here are some key tasks to focus on:

Conduct a final review of all event logistics: Once all the arrangements are in place, it is imperative to confirm and reconfirm the details with all vendors and suppliers.

Verify schedules, delivery times, equipment requirements, and other relevant details to confirm that the event team is on the same page.

Confirm audio-visual and technology: Double-check that all audio-visual and technology needs have been met, including equipment and testing.

Confirm food and beverage needs: Double and triple-confirm all catering arrangements and communicate any changes to the caterer or venue. Additionally, make sure to address all attendee dietary restrictions and allergens adequately.

Confirm Transportation needs: After booking transportation for your attendees and VIPs, confirm all arrangements well before the event. Double-check pick-up and drop-off times, confirm the number of vehicles required, and address special requests or requirements.

By confirming transportation arrangements ahead of time you will minimize potential disruptions or delays.

Confirm Security needs: Double-check any security needs, including hiring third-party personnel or coordinating with venue security.

Finalize your event seating plan: Take the time to assess VIP accommodations and verify seating arrangements while communicating any changes to your team and vendors. By having a well-planned seating plan, you can improve the flow of your event and make it easier for attendees to navigate the space.

Develop your event signage and banners: Create and print directional signage and banners to help attendees navigate the event and promote your brand.

On **event day**, all of your planning and preparation should come together to create a seamless experience for attendees. Here are some areas to pay attention to:

Set up the event venue and signage: Ensure event branding and signage are in place and set up appropriately, including event banners, directional signs, and other promotional materials.

Conduct audio-visual or technology checks: Test all audio-visual equipment, including microphones, speakers, projectors, and screens, to avoid any malfunctions.

Confirm all catering, deliveries, and transportation arrangements: Check with vendors to guarantee that all catering, deliveries, and transportation arrangements are on schedule and set up according to plan.

Manage event registration and ticketing: Make sure that the registration and ticketing process runs smoothly and that attendees receive their badges, wristbands, or tickets without any issues.

Manage event security and emergency response: Ensuring the safety of all attendees should be a top priority for any event. It is crucial to have well-trained security personnel who are fully aware of their roles and responsibilities. Moreover, emergency response procedures must be established and communicated clearly to all staff, volunteers, and attendees.

Adequate preparation must be taken to provide all equipment, such as first aid kits, fire extinguishers, and other commonly used medical supplies like OTC pain relievers.

Manage event clean-up and load-out:

1. After the event, engage the clean-up crew to remove equipment and materials from the venue.

2. Tear down any event structures, remove signage, and leave the venue in good condition.

3. Plan a final walk-through before leaving the property.

In the **post-event** phase, conduct a debrief and review to analyze the event's success and identify areas for improvement. Review attendee feedback, financial reports, and other metrics measured during the event. Use this data to make improvements for future events and adjust the event planning process as needed.

Send out event surveys or polls to attendees to gather valuable insights into what attendees liked and disliked about the event and ideas for future events. Follow up with attendees, sponsors, and partners to thank them for their support and gather any additional feedback.

Update the event website and marketing materials, including all outdated information. Evaluating the event's success and adjusting the event planning process as needed is crucial for continued success and growth in the future.

Run of Show

We talked briefly about the Run of Show (ROS) in a previous chapter, but I'd like to dive deeper into the importance of this document. It is truly the lifeline between you and all of your event team. A good Run of Show has a highly detailed breakdown of each segment of your event.

There are several reasons why having a ROS is will help you produce a successful event:

Provides structure: A detailed ROS makes allocating resources and managing the event flow easy, from the pre-event set-up to the post-event wrap-up. It minimizes confusion and helps everyone involved in the event know their responsibilities and the timeline for each segment. You can proactively address any issues before they arise by identifying potential bottlenecks or areas needing extra attention.

Helps with time management: A Run of Show serves as a blueprint for the event, outlining the timing and flow of each key component and activity. It reduces the risk of unexpected delays or setbacks.

A clear and detailed ROS allows the event team to prioritize tasks, allocate resources, and coordinate with various stakeholders with ease.

Whether managing the stage schedule, overseeing vendor set-up, or ensuring attendees have access to food and drinks, a Run of Show is a must-have tool that helps the event team stay on track and deliver a successful event.

Ensures smooth transitions: A Run of Show (ROS) allows your team to allocate the right amount of time to each segment of the event and avoid overrunning or underutilizing time slots. Moreover, it provides a clear overview of the event timeline, making it easier for the team to coordinate and make real-time adjustments as the event progresses.

By having a well-structured ROS in place, the event team can be confident that everything will run smoothly and efficiently, delivering a seamless experience for attendees. It will keep the event on track and maintain the desired pace, allowing them to adjust and make changes on the fly.

Facilitates communication: Having a clear and detailed plan, the event team can quickly identify and resolve any issues that arise without affecting the flow and success of the event. The Run of Show can guide rehearsals and pre-event planning to work out any kinks before event day.

Helps with contingency planning: An effectively planned and organized ROS can reduce stress and anxiety for the event team. By clearly understanding the event timeline and expectations at each step, the team can feel more relaxed and confident, leading to a more successful event, resulting in a more focused and efficient team better equipped to handle unexpected challenges and changes that may arise during the event.

Segments: A clear and organized structure for your event is crucial for success. By breaking down the event into smaller segments, you can focus on each element individually and ensure that it is planned and executed to the best of your ability.

For example, you can dedicate time and resources to making the registration process efficient and welcoming for attendees, craft engaging and informative opening remarks, and secure keynote speakers who will captivate and inspire your audience.

Similarly, you can plan interactive and informative breakout sessions, provide healthy and enjoyable meal options, and create opportunities for attendees to network and connect.

Speakers and Presenters: Including each speaker's information in the ROS is crucial. This information should consist of introductions, transitions, and any special requirements for entrance music, lighting, and microphone they may have. By including these details, the event team can properly introduce each speaker and display their presentation, including lighting and sound, to avoid technical or logistical issues.

Moreover, including speaker information in the ROS can help the event team prepare for any questions or discussions that may arise during the event. The ROS will enable the team to address concerns quickly and efficiently, creating a more engaging and interactive experience for attendees.

Technical Requirements: Detailed information on the timing and set-up of all audio-visual components in the ROS should include lighting, sound checks, and mic types for each presenter, as well as confirmation that multimedia presentations are uploaded to facilitate the technical aspects of the event.

Including this information in the ROS enables the event team to adequately prepare for the technical aspects and enhance the overall event experience by avoiding technical issues and delays. This, in turn, improves attendee engagement and satisfaction.

Contingency Plans: A contingency plan is essential to ensuring a successful event. By anticipating potential challenges and having contingency plans, the event team can promptly respond and resolve any issues, minimizing any negative impact on the event experience for attendees. Additionally, having a contingency plan reduces stress and uncertainty for the AV team, allowing them to focus on executing the event to the best of their abilities.

A minute-by-minute Run of Show is more than just a schedule; it's the backbone of any successful event. A ROS safeguards against overlooking critical details so things can easily go right. A Run of Show ensures that every aspect of the event is accounted for and executed seamlessly by providing a clear timeline and outline of responsibilities.

Having an organized planning system is crucial for the success of an event. It allows for efficient and effective coordination of various elements such as vendor management, event logistics, and communication with stakeholders. With a clear plan and timeline, potential issues can be identified and addressed proactively, leading to a more seamless and memorable event experience for attendees.

Mastering the Art of Negotiation: Strategies for Securing the Best Deals in Event Planning

Several things that may need to be negotiated for an event, depending on the specifics of the event. Some examples include:

Venue rental fees: Venue rental fees are a necessary component when it comes to event planning. When renting a venue, there are often different fees to account for. For example, some venues charge a flat rental fee, while others charge by the hour or day. You need to understand the fees associated with the venue rental and negotiate so you get a fair price.

An example of additional venue charges would be a cleaning fee or a security deposit that may be refundable. Other venues may charge a fee for specific equipment or services, such as audio-visual equipment, lighting, or catering services.

When negotiating venue rental fees, account for factors such as the event date, the time of day, and the duration. Sometimes, you can negotiate a lower rental price if you're willing to hold your event on a weekday or during an off-peak time.

You should evaluate the quality of service offered by the venue. For example, some venues provide event planning services, while others may provide catering or other services. The level of service provided may affect the rental fee, so it's important to negotiate these services as part of the complete fee structure.

Food and beverage costs: Food and beverage costs are a considerable part of an event budget and can vary widely depending on the type of event, menu selections, and guest count. Negotiate these costs upfront so they align with your budget and event goals. Be sure to discuss menu options and any dietary restrictions or preferences with the catering company to accommodate all guests.

It might benefit you to negotiate the option to bring in outside vendors or beverages to reduce costs or provide more variety for guests. Remember that any changes or additions to the menu may affect the total cost, so promptly communicate any updates to the catering company.

Audio-visual and technology fees: Audio-visual and technology fees are a part of the event budget. Depending on the type of event and its objectives, you may need to rent equipment such as microphones, speakers, projectors, and lighting to ensure that your attendees can hear and see everything. You may also need a team of professionals to set up and operate the equipment during the event.

It is crucial to negotiate these costs with the vendor or supplier. Take into consideration the event's length and complexity. You may get a discount on equipment rentals by bundling them together or negotiating a package deal that includes the services of the audio-visual team.

Account for any additional fees that may be incurred, such as overtime charges or last-minute changes to equipment needs. By negotiating these costs ahead of time and clearly understanding what is included in the fees, you can avoid any unexpected expenses that could blow your budget.

Speaker or entertainment fees: When planning an event, negotiate prices with any speakers or entertainment that will be a part of the event. These fees may vary depending on the popularity and demand of the speaker or entertainer and the length of their appearance or performance.

Negotiate in advance to understand what is expected from the speaker or entertainment, the venue, and what you are required to provide, including their appearance or performance time, travel and accommodation expenses, and any other specific requirements they may have.

When negotiating with speakers or entertainers for an event, discuss what will happen if they cannot perform as agreed. Include clauses for cancellation fees or the ability to reschedule the performance for a later date.

It's a good idea to discuss what will happen if the speaker or entertainer is unable to fulfill their obligations due to unforeseen circumstances, such as illness or travel disruptions. It is prudent to have a backup plan to ensure the event can continue as smoothly as possible.

Negotiating speaker or entertainment fees early in the planning process can keep costs within budget while allowing for a high-quality and engaging event as well as establishing positive working relationships for future events.

Transportation costs: Transportation costs can vary greatly depending on the event's size and location. Negotiating transportation costs can include securing transportation for attendees, speakers, and event staff. You may need to arrange shuttle services, rental cars, flights, and hotels for out-of-town guests.

Account for transportation costs early in the event planning process, as they can significantly affect the budget. Negotiating transportation costs may involve working with a transportation vendor to secure discounted rates or dealing with hotels for shuttle services.

Determine permits or licenses for transportation services, such as permits for shuttle buses or rental car services. By carefully negotiating transportation costs and planning for transportation needs ahead of time, event planners can provide a smooth and efficient transportation experience for all attendees and staff.

As an added comfort level, negotiating outsourcing rates for local transportation vendors, like car services, motorcoaches, or other people movers, can increase the chances that the vendor can fulfill the event's needs, even in unexpected circumstances. Look at the number of attendees, the distance between the airport, hotel, and venue, and any specific transportation needs, such as wheelchair accessibility.

Decor and signage costs: Decor and signage costs are a staple of event planning and should be accounted for during negotiation. Decor can include everything from floral arrangements and centerpieces to lighting and furniture rentals. Decor pieces might consist of entrance ways, step and repeats, and interactive stations for attendees to engage with. Signage can include everything from directional signs to branding and sponsorship signage.

When negotiating decor and signage costs, be clear about your budget and what you expect to receive. Be specific about the type of decor and signage you want, and ask for a breakdown of costs.

Try to work with vendors who offer package deals or discounts for bulk orders so you stay within your budget while still achieving the look and feel you want for your event.

Review all contracts carefully and make sure they include details such as delivery, set up, and take down of decor and signage. Address compensation if they fail to deliver all elements for the event.

Vendor and supplier fees: When organizing an event, you may need to hire vendors and suppliers to provide various services such as catering, audio-visual equipment, transportation, and decor.

When negotiating vendor and supplier fees, clearly communicate your budget and expectations. Ask for a detailed breakdown of costs to verify no hidden fees or additional charges exist. Negotiate a payment schedule that works for both parties.

Try to negotiate a discount for booking multiple services with the same vendor or supplier. For example, if you are hiring a catering company, ask if they offer a discount for providing or the other rental equipment.

Review vendor and supplier contracts carefully before signing; make sure you understand all of the terms and conditions, including cancellation policies and any penalties for late payments or changes to the agreement.

Advertising and marketing expenses: Advertising and marketing expenses are a part of event planning, as they create buzz and attract attendees. These costs include promotional materials, social media advertising, print and digital ads, and sponsorships. Negotiate these expenses with vendors and suppliers so that you get the best possible value for your budget.

When negotiating advertising and marketing expenses, closely examine the audience you are targeting and the most effective ways to reach them. Work with vendors and suppliers to develop creative and engaging marketing materials that will capture your audience's attention and encourage them to attend your event.

Evaluating the potential return on investment (ROI) for each marketing expense is smart. For example, sponsorships can provide valuable exposure and networking opportunities but may come at a high cost. Work with sponsors to negotiate the terms of the sponsorship and stay in alignment with your event goals and objectives.

Insurance and permit costs: Insurance and permits are a crucial part of any event and are often overlooked. Factor in the cost of event insurance to protect against any accidents or incidents that may occur during the event. Note permits may be required from local government agencies for events in public spaces or involving road closures.

Be proactive when negotiating insurance and permit costs, outline the specific requirements for your event, and work with a knowledgeable insurance broker or permitting agency to ensure that you have adequate coverage and all required permits.

Remember that insurance and permit costs can vary widely depending on the location and size of the event, as well as the specific requirements of the event venue and local government agencies. Budget accordingly and to factor in any additional costs that may arise during the permitting process.

Staff and volunteer compensation: When planning an event, including payment for the staff, contractors, and volunteers working the event in order to stay within your budget. Compensation includes their salary and any additional costs, such as meals, lodging, and transportation.

For paid staff and contractors, negotiate their fees and include any overtime pay or bonuses for exceptional work. Be sure to have an explicit agreement outlining their responsibilities and expectations.

For volunteers, offer incentives such as free admission to the event, exclusive access to certain areas, or recognition for their work. Communicate their roles and responsibilities, and provide training and support.

Budgeting for compensation in your total event budget can be expensive. By properly compensating your team, you can keep your team motivated, committed, and focused on delivering a successful event.

Each line item's percentage of an event budget can vary widely depending on the specific event, its size, and its location.

However, generally speaking, the breakdown might look like this:

→ Venue rental fees: 20-30%

→ Catering and beverage costs: 20-30%

→ audio-visual and technology fees: 10-15%

→ Speaker or entertainment fees: 10-15%

→ Transportation costs: 5-10%

→ Decor and signage costs: 5-10%

→ Vendor and supplier fees: 5-10%

→ Advertising and marketing expenses: 5-10%

→ Insurance and permit costs: 2-5%

→ Staff and volunteer compensation: 2-5%

Note that these percentages can shift based on the priorities and goals of the event. For example, an event in a high-cost city or with specialized equipment needs may have higher prices for specific line items.

Refining your negotiation skills can reduce costs by allowing your event planning team to:

Understand the market: Knowing the pricing and options available from vendors and suppliers helps negotiate a better deal.

For example, if you're looking to book a caterer for your event, research and gather information on the pricing and services offered by various caterers in the area. Therefore, you'll understand reasonable and competitive pricing for their services.

You can negotiate discounts or added services by showing them that you have done your research and know what other vendors offer.

Create competition: Negotiating with multiple vendors/suppliers and creating competition among them can decrease prices.

For example, let's say you're negotiating with a catering company for your event. You've researched and found that other catering companies in the area offer similar services for a lower price.

You can use this knowledge to negotiate a better deal with the catering company you're interested in. You might say, "I've done some research and found that other catering companies in the area offer similar services for a lower price. Can you match their price or offer additional services to make up the difference?" Using your market knowledge, you can negotiate a better deal and save money on catering costs.

Bundle services: Combining multiple services from a single vendor/supplier can result in a discounted price.

An example of bundling services can be when negotiating with an audio-visual company. Instead of hiring different lighting and sound companies, you can deal with the audio-visual company to provide both services, resulting in a bundled discount.

Negotiate contracts: Negotiating the terms and conditions of contracts with vendors/suppliers can lead to a better price, flexible payment terms, and other concessions.

For example, negotiating with a hotel for a room block for your event can result in a better rate per room and more favorable cancellation policies.

You can negotiate with a catering company for an event, including the menu options, the number of courses, and the price per person. By arranging these terms, you can get a lower cost per person or include additional courses for the same price.

Negotiating payment terms may allow for a more flexible payment schedule, such as paying a portion of the fee upfront and the remainder after the event.

Be prepared to walk away: Being willing to walk away from a negotiation if the terms are not favorable can often lead to better offers from the vendor/supplier.

For example, suppose a vendor is quoting a price that is above your budget but knows that other vendors in the market are charging less for the same service. In that case, you can negotiate with them and mention that you have other options. This approach can cause them to reconsider their initial quote and offer you a better deal to win your business. If they are still unwilling to budge on the price, you can be prepared to walk away and find a more affordable vendor. This approach can put you in a stronger position during negotiations and save you money in the long run.

Good negotiation skills can result in major savings for an event and allow the event planner to stay within their budget while still delivering a high-quality event.

Building a Strong Support System: The Importance of Collaboration in Event Planning

C hoose partners who share your vision and goals for the event and can bring their expertise and resources to create a successful and memorable experience.

Collaborating with partners with a proven track record in their respective fields can provide peace of mind and reduce stress during planning.

Here are some potential partners you can collaborate with:

Event planners: These professionals have the expertise and experience to assist you with planning and executing a flawless event. They can handle everything from venue selection, vendor management, and day-of coordination.

Marketing agencies: Collaborating with a marketing agency to promote your event to the right audience and maximize attendance can be a huge time saver and free you up to focus on more essential duties. They can assist you with creating a marketing plan, developing promotional materials, and executing social media campaigns.

Production companies: If you need help with audio-visual, lighting, or stage design, a production company can be a great partner. They can guide you through creating a memorable and transformative experience for attendees.

Food and beverage companies: Food and beverage is often a highlight of any event. Collaborating with a reputable catering company can ensure your guests are satisfied and leave a positive impression of your event.

Entertainment agencies: If you want to add excitement and engagement to your event, working with an entertainment agency can provide you with various options, such as keynote speakers, musicians, or comedians.

Technology companies: Technology can enhance the experience of your event, from check-in to live streaming to interactive displays. Collaborating with a technology company can help you integrate the latest technology into your event.

Nonprofit organizations: Collaborating with a nonprofit organization can help you achieve your event goals and give back to the community—partner with a nonprofit that aligns with your values and event theme when possible.

If you host your event locally, creating partnerships and collaborations with local vendors is beneficial because it can benefit both parties and make the event planning process much smoother. Local vendors can provide expertise and knowledge about the area that can be invaluable to event planners. They can offer cost-effective solutions for services and products for the event.

By partnering with local vendors, you can create a mutually beneficial relationship where they can promote your event and attract attendees. You can support their business and increase their visibility within the community.

Local vendors can provide personalization and customization that may not be possible with more prominent, impersonal vendors.

Moreover, working with local vendors can create a sense of community and local pride. By showcasing local businesses and talent, you can create a unique and memorable experience for attendees while supporting the local economy.

However, if you frequently take your events to different destinations. Having a handful of key partners willing to travel with you may be worthwhile as it will provide consistency and familiarity with your event, especially regarding logistics and operations.

For example, having a trusted audio-visual team familiar with your event's set-up and requirements can streamline the planning and execution, even in unfamiliar locations.

And as a bonus, having key partners willing to travel with you can also foster stronger relationships and collaboration, leading to better communication and problem-solving during the event.

Event Planning Resources

101 Questions to Ask to Build a Highly Defined Avatar:

This workbook will walk you through 101 questions to help you get to know the people you serve in your business and through your events.

https://www.bankableevents.com/101-questions-to-ask

Event Planning Checklist:

Here is a basic event planning checklist that includes key tasks and considerations for planning and executing a successful event:

https://www.bankableevents.com/event-planning-checklist

Sponsorship and Sponsorship Packages:

Do you need to recruit sponsors for your upcoming event?

Check out our Sponsorship Pitch Deck Template. This eleven-slide deck will walk you through the primary information potential sponsors want to know before agreeing to sponsor your event.

https://www.bankableevents.com/event-sponsorship-pitch-deck

Need assistance putting together your sponsorship packages? Follow the link below to see our **Sponsorship Package Samples**:

https://www.bankableevents.com/sponsorship-package-samples

Conclusion

I am thrilled to have shared "Master the Art of Planning Live Events - A Small Business Owners Guide to Build Your Brand, Drive Revenue, and Grow a Sustainable Business" with you. I hope and pray that it helps you navigate the dynamic and exciting world of leveraging the power of live events to grow your business. My goal is to equip you with the knowledge and practical skills to create memorable experiences for your guests.

Being flexible and adaptive to changing circumstances is crucial as a small business owner. Always remember to embrace technology and innovations that can streamline your processes and enhance attendees' experience. Staying true to your vision and consistently delivering exceptional events will establish a solid reputation and set your business apart in this competitive industry.

Moreover, always appreciate the importance of self-improvement and continuous learning. The event industry is constantly evolving. To stay ahead of the curve, keeping updated on the latest trends, technologies, and best practices is vital.

As you embark on your event planning journey, remember that you are not just creating events; you are crafting experiences that have the power to inspire, educate, and entertain. With passion, determination, and valuable insights from this book, you and your small business are well on your way to mastering the art of planning live events.

May your events bring joy and lasting memories to all who attend, and may your success as an event host and small business owner be a testament to your hard work, creativity, and dedication.

Good luck, and here's to a future filled with unforgettable live events!

Anza's Recommended Reading

he Big Leap: Conquer Your Hidden Fear and Take Life to the Next Level by Gay Hendrix focuses on helping individuals overcome self-limiting beliefs and fears that prevent them from achieving their full potential. Hendricks introduces the concept of the "Upper Limit Problem," which refers to the self-imposed barriers people create in their lives due to fear, guilt, or other negative emotions. By identifying these barriers and learning how to break through them, readers can unlock their true potential and experience tremendous success, happiness, and fulfillment in all aspects of life.

The 15 Invaluable Laws of Growth: Live Then and Reach Your Full Potential by John Maxwell - One of my favorite books for personal growth and development. By understanding and applying these laws, individuals can unlock their potential and succeed in various life aspects.

The 12 Week Year by Brian P. Moran and Michael Lennington - A guide to help individuals and organizations improve their productivity and achieve their goals by focusing on 12-week cycles instead of traditional annual plans.

Acknowledgments

I want to extend my deepest gratitude to…

Gary Lydic for inviting me to be part of a fantastic event-planning team. Working alongside you opened my eyes to the immense potential of events in transforming lives and creating a far-reaching impact beyond what we could achieve individually.

To Kathy Fort-Carty and Susan Fort, I am forever grateful for the chance you took on me over 20 years ago. Your mentorship and high standards pushed me beyond my comfort zone, allowing me to thrive and grow in the world of event planning.

Malahni Ake, I am grateful for your constant friendship and unwavering belief in my abilities. Your encouragement to do more, give more, and serve more has led to the creation of this book – a testament to the power of saying YES to life-changing collaborations.

To Pat Miller, thank you for opening the door to the possibility of teaching beyond event planning and stepping into my zone of genius. Your insights have inspired me to develop strategies that uniquely serve the small business community.

Jim Edwards for his incredible copywriting mentorship. Your unwavering encouragement and guidance gave me the courage to embark on this solo book-writing journey. The weekly mentoring and training you provided have been truly transformative in shaping my approach to writing.

Lastly, my heartfelt thanks go to Danica Trebel for helping me break free from my thoughts and put them down on paper. Your gentle nudging and support were instrumental in bringing this book to fruition.

About the Author

*A*nza Goodbar is a serial entrepreneur, dedicated mother, and passionate grandmother. With her boundless energy, creativity, and determination, Anza has built a successful career spanning multiple industries while maintaining a deep connection to her family and passions.

As the proud mother of four exceptional grown children, Anza has always been a supportive and loving role model. Her commitment to her family extends to her role as a doting grandmother to an incredible granddaughter, cherishing every moment they spend together.

Anza's adventurous spirit shines through outside her entrepreneurial pursuits and family life. She has an insatiable love for hiking, she has summited three 14ers (peaks with summits above 14,000 feet). Her zest for life extends to the dance floor, where she gracefully showcases her ballroom and Latin dance skills, a hobby that allows her to express her creativity and love for movement.

With a strong belief in the importance of work-life balance, Anza prioritizes spending quality time with her family, creating cherished memories that will last a lifetime. Her unwavering dedication to her loved ones, her businesses, and her personal growth inspires all who know her.

Through her journey as an entrepreneur, mother, and grandmother, Anza Goodbar has mastered the art of living life to the fullest. Her story serves as a testament to the power of hard work, perseverance, and the love of family.

Events Convert Academy

We offer FREE Live training each month to help small business owners learn how to leverage the power of live events to grow their business. Follow the link below to sign up for one of our next Masterclass:

https://www.bankableevents.com/events-convert-academy

C.R.U.S.H. Your Way to Success
5 Things You Need to Know to Host a Life Event That Converts Leads into Paying Clients (without experience)

From Planning to Profit:
S.C.A.L.E. Your Business with Live Events

Follow us on LinkedIn:
https://www.linkedin.com/in/anzagoodbar/

Join our new Facebook group:
https://www.facebook.com/groups/bankableeventsforsmallbusinesses

CPSIA information can be obtained
at www.ICGtesting.com
Printed in the USA
BVHW050418260423
663005BV00015B/904

9 798218 189174